y David Lewis include:

n (Methuen)
wn Mind (Penguin/Holt Reinhart)
: Peak Performance Past Forty (Methuen)
bathing: The Puzzle of Personal Attraction (Constable)
tress Management (Secker and Warburg)
nguage of Success (Bantam)
er (Holt Reinhart)

WINI
NE
BUSII

Other books

The Alpha P
Know Your
Life Unlimit
Loving and
One Minute
The Secret L
Thinking Be

WINNING *NEW* BUSINESS

A practical guide to successful sales presentations

Dr DAVID LEWIS

First published in 1993 by
Judy Piatkus (Publishers) Ltd of
5 Windmill Street, London W1P 1HF

A catalogue record for this book is
available from the British Library

ISBN 0-7499-1222-7

Edited by Carol Franklin
Designed by Chris Warner
Artwork by Chris Willet/The Image Factory

Set in 11/13 pt Compugraphic Times by
Action Typesetting Limited, Gloucester

Printed and bound in Great Britain by
Mackays of Chatham PLC, Chatham, Kent

ACKNOWLEDGEMENTS

This part of any book reminds me of credits glimpsed at the end of blockbuster films as you hurry from the cinema. Who wants or needs to know the names of the key grip, matte artist or Best Boy?

With academic papers lavish acknowledgements can be even more suspect. 'I am overwhelmingly grateful to Professor Blot for allowing me access to his original research . . .' may mean no more than 'I have plagiarised poor old Blot mercilessly and only hope by this display of grovelling to avoid a letter from his lawyers.'

The following votes of thanks, however, owe nothing to either convention or legal consequences. I am sincerely grateful to the large number of people who made the writing of this book possible.

In particular to my research associate Melanie Whitehouse for conducting the interviews. And to those presentation specialists from advertising, public relations and industry who generously gave their time to be interviewed especially – and in alphabetical order – Peter Bingle, John Cousins, Paul Cowan, Denis Horton, Graham Lancaster, Charles Makin, Rex Stewart and Basil Towers.

My thanks to colleagues at the David Lewis Consultancy, particularly managing director Cynthia Hemming, for helpful suggestions and forbearance in tolerating my foul mood while writing the book.

Chris Willet of The Image Factory created the illustrations.

Finally my thanks to Gill Cormode, editorial director at Piatkus, for her advice, patience and encouragement during this book's elephantine gestation period.

CONTENTS

STAGE FIVE Creating Lifetime Customer Loyalty

HOW WELL DO YOU SELL?

This quick but powerful test will help you to identify your key strengths when making a sales presentation.

Simply choose the symbol which you feel best represents your personality. Your immediate response is the most reliable one.

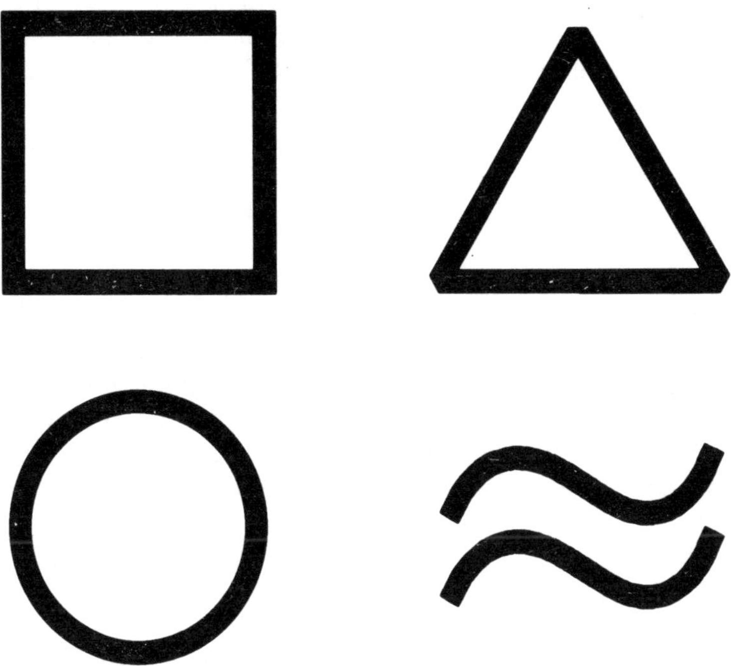

To learn what your choice reveals, turn the page.

What Your Sale Symbol Reveals

Square

Your approach to sales presentations is logical and methodical. But you sometimes lack sensitivity to the emotional needs of your customers. In Stage Three of this book you will discover ways of capturing hearts as well as minds when winning new business.

Triangle

Determination and persistence characterise your sales presentations. But you may be insufficiently flexible when identifying the extent of your product benefits. This could blind you to new business opportunities. Expand your creative potential by following the practical advice I provide in Stage Two of this book.

Circle

Friendly and sociable, you have a natural talent for selling. With the squiggle, this is one of the two most popular choices for sales professionals. One snag – you may not always be tough enough when closing the deal after an otherwise excellent sales presentation. To learn powerful closes which will help you secure that new business, see Stage Four of this book.

Squiggle

You excel at motivating and inspiring others by your sales presentations. With the circle, this is one of the two most popular symbols for sales professionals. But you could find it hard to develop lasting relationships with your clients. Stage five offers practical guidance in this powerful method of finding more new business to win.

Later in this book I shall explain how and why this test works, and show you how the other insights it provides can give you the psychological edge when winning new business.

How to Get the Best from this Book

Because every business and every customer is so different, there can never be any cookbook formula which guarantees selling success.

Successful sales presentations are individually crafted to meet the expectations and needs of those customers for whom they are intended.

This applies not only to face-to-face presentations, of course, but to all forms of promotion where, thanks to sophisticated databases, targeting precise segments of the market is becoming increasingly possible.

The fox, it is said, knows many things, while the hedgehog knows just one big thing.

Winning new business in an uncertain world means adopting the strategy of the fox rather than that of the hedgehog.

My advice is to take from this book whatever ideas, insights and procedures are best suited to your current needs, while keeping in mind the importance of a flexible approach to developing your winning sales strategies.

INTRODUCTION: WE ARE ALL IN THE BUSINESS OF SELLING

'EVERYONE lives by selling something.'
Robert Louis Stevenson

NO MATTER what business you are in, if you want to succeed you must also be in the business of selling.

This holds true whatever the size of your company or the nature of its business. It applies as much to family firms as to multinationals, to long-established enterprises as well as brand new start-ups.

Selling should be of as great a concern to people offering professional services, such as accountants, architects and artists, as it already is to manufacturers and retailers.

In a fiercely competitive global market place the alternatives are as straightforward as they are stark.

Sell your products or services more energetically, efficiently and successfully than your rivals, and you will flourish.

Fail to win new business and you will rapidly flounder.

Long gone are the days when any company is able even to survive, let alone prosper, by offering a better product or superior service than their rivals.

The graveyard of failed firms and bankrupt businesses is filled to overflowing with companies which, despite providing high-quality products and services, rapidly perished as a result of fatal flaws in their selling.

This is *not* to suggest that quality can ever be compromised. The global dominance of consumer electronics by Japanese manufacturers has clearly shown the value of assured quality in securing intense consumer loyalty.

But offering first-class products or services is rarely sufficient to secure you lucrative new business in the first instance. For that you must have an equally exceptional sales strategy.

The Presentation Pyramid

There are many ways in which companies can present products or services to their target market. The pyramid overleaf illustrates these different layers from broadcast media to sales presentations.

As we move up the pyramid the cost per individual customer increases. Which form of promotion is chosen, therefore, depends on the relationship between profit and cost for each method. Producers of mass market consumer goods concentrate their spending at the lower end of the pyramid, while business-to-business marketing can involve all the available presentation techniques.

Although the term 'sales presentations' could be applied to any promotion which draws attention to your product or service – from hand-written fliers announcing a local car boot sale to million pound television commercials – this book concentrates on face-to-face and business-to-business selling. Such presentations have three distinguishing features.

The first is that they have the highest cost per customer of any marketing options.

Taking into account direct and indirect expenses, not even the cheapest face-to-face visit can be made for less than £500, while the majority of presentations demand far greater expenditure. Some pitches by advertising agencies, for example, cost tens of thousands of pounds. Even with more modest presentations, when one adds to the equation those presentations which fail to result in orders, the true cost rapidly escalates.

This means that face-to-face presentations must always be reserved for customers whose lifetime spend is likely to greatly exceed your total sales investment.

This also underscores the crucial importance of hitting the target as often as possible. The only way to do this is to approach every stage of the process in a thorough and thoroughly professional manner.

Secondly, sales presentations are also expensive for your prospective customers. One or more of their, often senior, employees must attend, and if the presentation takes place at their premises they bear the additional costs of lighting, heating and accommodation. Even when the presentation is held in your offices they still incur travel expenses.

Provided your customers feel they have received a fair return on their investment this is acceptable. But should the sales presentation seem irrelevant and/or needlessly time-consuming, considerable resentment is created. This not only makes it less likely you will win their business on that occasion, but significantly reduces your chances of successful sales in the future.

Thirdly, despite their high expense and possible risks, presentations remain the most successful method of winning profitable new business.

As Table 1 shows, face-to-face sales presentations are rated as more persuasive than all other forms of promotion. The only method rated equally effective is that of personal recommendation.

Table 1: *Methods for winning new business*

Activity	Rating
Positive recommendations	5.3
New business presentations	5.3
Personal contact	4.7
Publicity on successful campaigns	4.2
Sales calls	3.2
Trade advertising	3.3
Direct mail	3.1
Unsolicited proposals	2.8

Adapted from the *Journal of Advertising Research*, Vol. 32, No. 5, September/October 1992, pp. 10–15.

In my view a key element in any successful presentation is to develop relationships with your customers which guarantee such recommendations. In this sense, therefore, they are a part and parcel of winning new business.

To obtain his data James R. Wills, professor of marketing and international business at the University of Hawaii's College of Business Administration, polled 2,686 firms with annual advertising budgets in excess of $500,000. Directors of advertising were asked to rate eight ways of winning new business on a scale, where 7 = 'Very effective' and 1 = 'Not effective at all'.

The promotional methods surveyed were:

1. personal contact with top management – the 'old boy network';
2. positive recommendations by satisfied clients;
3. publicity on recent successful campaigns;
4. responding to requests for new business presentations;
5. trade advertising;
6. direct mail;
7. unsolicited speculative proposals;
8. new business presentations.

While some managers believe that being on good terms with senior executives, playing golf with their vice-presidents or going to the same school as the chairperson of prospective customers will win them the business, those in the best position to evaluate this old boy network remain sceptical.

Cold calling, direct mail and trade advertising receive a medium to low rating which, not surprisingly perhaps, with unsolicited and speculative proposals are rated the least effective ways of finding new business.

But, although potential customers consider sales presentations the most effective form of promotions, this is not to dismiss or denigrate other promotional methods. As Professor Wills makes clear, when the same evaluations were made by advertising agency bosses, as opposed to the buyers of their wares, those who enjoyed greatest success at winning new business rated *all* eight methods higher than did their less successful competitors.

This book is concerned solely with selling via face-to-face presentations, whether on a one-to-one basis or between buying and selling teams from the would-be supplier and the prospective consumer.

Its purpose is to provide you with the knowledge and practical techniques needed to create sales presentations that are sufficiently persuasive and creative to win new business against tough competition.

The Five Stages of Winning Presentation

Winning sales presentations involve far more than merely displaying your products or services to potential buyers.

The face-to-face visit represents only one stage in a sales strategy encompassing every aspect of your company's philosophy, outlook and performance.

In an activity as psychologically complex as selling, no one element can ever be usefully or realistically isolated from the rest of the sales process.

This means that to write a practical guide which concentrated solely on that period spent in direct contact with clients would be to tell only part of the story. It would prove about as much help as writing a driving manual that explained only how to start and steer the car!

Companies which sell most successfully are not just good at selling. They are good at everything!

For this reason I shall describe hands-on techniques for enhancing every stage in devising and following through effective sales presentations. These include:

- finding new customers whose business it will be possible and worthwhile to win;

- identifying the particular needs and matching them to the benefits your company is able to offer;
- developing a sales presentation which will demonstrate your ability to match their needs in the most persuasive manner possible;
- making the actual presentation confidently and in a style tailored to the psychological needs and expectations of your audience;
- developing a lasting relationship with the customer so that you can both enjoy a maximum return on your investment of time, effort and energy in winning their business and generate new business opportunities through hot leads and word-of-mouth recommendations.

As the illustration below shows these five stages of selling are best compared to closely meshed cogs, each driving the next in line to produce a perpetually turning sales machine.

Selling to Win

On both sides of the Atlantic and around the Pacific Basin, companies ranging in size from multinationals to family firms, and from long-established businesses to brand new start-ups, are expanding their market share and increasing their profits by forging an unbeatable alliance of quality allied to outstanding selling methods.

By doing so they are not only enjoying commercial success today but laying foundations on which to build even greater prosperity tomorrow.

Their secret lies in understanding the practical psychology behind creating sales presentations which can win the hearts, the minds and the business of new customers.

You can do the same.

This book will show you how.

STAGE ONE

Finding New Business

'A BUSINESS exists because the consumer is willing to pay you his money. You run a business to satisfy the consumer. That isn't marketing, that goes way beyond marketing.'

Peter F. Drucker

'WHEN the going gets tough, the tough get going!'

Joseph P. Kennedy

1 HOW BENEFITS BUILD YOUR BUSINESS

'CHRISTOPHER COLUMBUS set off without knowing where he was going. When he arrived he had no idea where he was. He came home without knowing where he'd been. And he paid for his trip with other people's money. Many businesses run on the same basis.'

Anonymous graffiti

THAT MESSAGE, which I saw not long ago scrawled on the cloakroom wall at a leading business school, nicely sums up the attitude of many people in business to the business they are in.

The power of their sales presentations is diminished, sometimes to the point of being almost entirely ineffective, by the fact that they have no clear idea, no shining vision, of where they are going, whether or not they have arrived or whereabouts they have been.

As a result their companies often resemble blindfolded individuals blundering around in a fog-filled room!

On other occasions I am reminded more of the drunk desperately searching for his lost keys beneath a street lamp, not because he had dropped them there but because 'the light was so much better'.

Like him these firms target their efforts not in the most profitable direction, but towards those goals most easily seen.

In order to find new business two points must first be clearly established.

The first thing to do is understand what business you are really in. This provides you with a clear course to steer.

Second, you must identify which segment of your target market offers the business that is most worth winning.

What Do You Really Sell?

Let me start by asking what might seem an absurd, obvious and even insulting question.

'What is it you actually sell?'

In my experience few businesspeople are fully aware of the true nature or purpose of their business.

Toothpaste manufacturers believe they sell toothpaste.

Travel agents assume they sell holidays.

The narrowness of such understanding represents a significant reason for losing sales and missing opportunities for new business. It is the reason why many start-ups fail and even established firms go to the wall.

If, seventy years ago, America's powerful railroad bosses had realised their real business was transporting people and goods they might have escaped bankruptcy by diversifying into the expanding market for air and motor travel.

The fact is nobody buys products.

They only buy benefits.

We purchase toothpaste not for the joy of owning a

tube, but to possess the benefits of healthy and attractive teeth.

We buy holidays to benefit from relaxation and the excitement of exotic new locations.

As the president of one of America's largest drill manufacturers commented recently: 'Last year we sold millions of ½in drill bits to people who did not need them. What they actually wanted and bought was the ability to drill ½in holes!'

ALMOST OUT FOR THE PUNCH

'Marketing Myopia' nearly caused IBM to miss out on the computer revolution. For decades Tom Watson Snr, Big Blue's founding father, regarded his company as being in the business of making and selling punched card machinery.

This recorded data by punching holes in cards the size of a dollar bill. Developed by a young Americal inventor, Herman Hollerith, in the 1880s, punched cards remained unchanged for more than seventy years and provided the foundations on which IBM arose.

In the early 1950s, full order books and healthy profits blinded Watson and his fellow executives to the significance of storing data on magnetic tape.

Only at the eleventh hour did they respond to customer complaints over the soaring storage costs for millions of punch cards by changing over to magnetic tape.

The crucial shift came with the realisation that IBM's real business was not selling punched card machines but the benefits of fast, accurate data processing.

Lesson: To win new business first clearly identify what business you are really in.

Benefits Not Features Make Fortunes

The art of winning new business is to provide a better match between the benefits a customer seeks and those your company can provide than is available from your competitors. Unfortunately, some salespeople appear to have difficulty distinguishing features from benefits.

As a result of their confusion many presentations focus on features, even though most customers only want to be told about benefits.

'This car has full air conditioning . . .'

'This camera has a top shutter speed of 1/2,000 second . . .'

'This suit is made from pure wool . . .'

Features are the physical attributes built into any product or service.

Benefits are the reasons why customers care about those features in the first place.

This emphasis on feature selling is most apparent in the presentations for such high-tech products as computers and fax machines. People selling these products are often technically minded themselves and assume their customers have sufficient knowledge to identify the benefits when told about the features.

Where a buyer has an equal, or superior, level of expertise to the seller this may well be true. But it is an assumption which could easily lead to lost business.

A computer buff who was told 'This machine has a 486 chip, 120 MB hard drive and 8 meg of RAM' would translate the specifications into the benefits of fast speed, ample storage and the ability to run memory-hungry programs, without difficulty. But for a less experienced business user, this shopping list of features might be so much off-putting jargon.

Even when the more obvious benefits are apparent to customers some of those which are less immediately apparent could be missed.

As I shall explain in Stage Four, for fact-oriented customers this type of presentation works reasonably well. If you picked the Square as your symbol in the test at the start of this book, it is likely you too enjoy being sold on features. Your logical mind prefers hard facts to emotional appeals.

But, except when selling a highly technical product to specialist customers, it is advisable to translate key features into benefits. And even when making sales presentations to specialists, some of the less obvious benefits are worth spelling out.

For most business customers and the majority of products, however, feature selling is insufficiently persuasive. To win customers' hearts you must translate intellectually appealing physical aspects into emotion-arousing benefits.

Changing Features to Benefits

To convert features to benefits all you have to do is complete the statement starting: 'Which means that . . .'

Suppose, for instance, you are sales manager of a courier company which has fifty despatch riders on duty around the clock.

Instead of assuming a prospective customer will immediately recognise the benefit this feature provides, you should illustrate it by painting a simple word picture: 'We have fifty despatch riders on duty around the clock *which means that* an experienced courier will always be on hand to collect your packages within ten minutes of the call.'

The Five Types of Benefits

There are five main types of benefits. These can arise either from the products being sold (**service outcome benefits**) or from the manner in which they are delivered (**service process benefits**).

Both types of benefit can be placed in one of five categories. Being able to identify which category a particular benefit comes into makes it easier to identify those of greatest relevance to a particular customer.

Standard Benefits

The most basic benefits of all, standard benefits stem from the nature of the product or service itself, and are common to every similar product or service. For example, all fax machines offer the standard benefit of speeding the transmission of documents. Every private security firm sells the benefit of protecting your property against theft and vandalism.

While standard benefits are seldom remarkable they may still need to be explained to customers unfamiliar with the type of product or service you provide.

Double Benefits

Two standard benefits can often be linked in order to create more persuasive selling points: 'We do all our own slide making and graphics in house (**standard benefit**) *which means that* we are able to offer a fast and reliable service (**double benefit**).'

Chained Benefits

Chained benefits can be used to pinpoint non-obvious advantages, often of special interest to a particular customer.

Chaining benefits can be a powerful way of tailoring

your sales presentation to the needs of individual clients. One way of applying a high level of creativity to this task is by constructing a **chaining tree** as illustrated below.

Here, some of the chained benefits of air conditioning in cars have been developed in ways which might appeal to two different types of motorist.

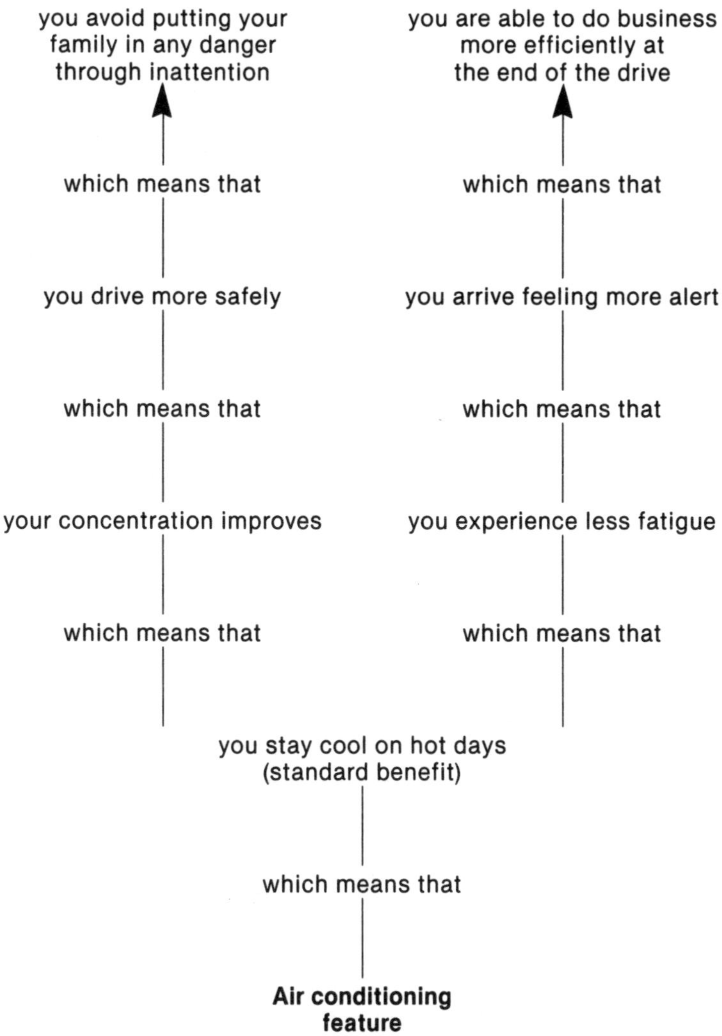

Business motorists might be attracted by the benefit of greater alertness when they arrive at their destination, while family drivers could feel that transporting their children more safely and in greater comfort was a significant benefit.

To create a chaining tree simply write down a key feature and then use the phrase 'which means that' as many times as possible to tease out all the benefits. When choosing a feature it is often best to start with those unique to your product or service, since these are the ones which differentiate you most clearly from competitors. Such features produce . . .

Unique Benefits

If, for example, your unique selling point (USP) was being the only telemarketing company to employ multilingual staff this differential benefit might be presented as: '. . . which means that we can deal courteously and efficiently with all your overseas telephone marketing requirements'.

The USP usually relates to some special feature, or features, of the goods on offer. However, where these are absent, or not relevant to a particular client, you may need to turn a feature of the company itself into a USP: 'We are the only office supplies company guaranteeing next-day, no charge, delivery on all orders, which means that you can reduce overheads by not having to stock large quantities of stationery.'

BUILDING PROFITS BY ADDING BENEFITS

Baxter International, an $8.9 billion a year hospital products company, saw an opportunity to increase profits by saving their customers time and money.

After learning of the high costs which

hospitals incurred in storing and distributing their products, Baxter developed Valuelink, a service which dramatically reduces inventory costs and improves distribution of supplies.

A hospital can delegate to Baxter the costly task of ensuring that essentials such as needles, bandages and syringes wind up in the right place and in the correct quantities.

To make this benefit work Baxter installed computer equipment in the hospital which sends information back to its own warehouse, on a daily basis, monitoring the exact quantities of every product used.

A service fee of 3 to 6 per cent of sales means higher profits and strong customer loyalty. From the buyers' viewpoint benefits include lower running costs and the guarantee that medical staff will always have sufficient supplies of life-saving equipment.

Lesson: Identifying and solving a genuine problem for your customer will benefit you both.

Company Benefits

So far we have looked at service outcome benefits. But to succeed your sales presentation must also include details of service process benefits. That is how customers can expect the product to be delivered. The key words here are:

- empathy
- responsiveness and
- assurance.

Increasingly these days customers are seeking long-term partnerships with their suppliers. Such a close relationship affords many benefits including assured reliability, the saving of time and money by eliminating any need for further sales presentations (see Chapter 2), and more relaxed day-to-day dealings with known individuals. They may also expect to enjoy a priority attention for their needs from suppliers depending on them for repeat business.

These service process benefits are every bit as relevant to winning new business – and central to ensuring customer loyalty (See Stage Five) – as service outcome benefits.

At the back of your customer's mind during your sales presentation will be such questions as:

> 'Does this company understand and share our corporate values?'
>
> 'Do they have the expertise to trouble-shoot problems directly with our technical staff?'

So it is essential to include in your sales presentations such reassuring comments as:

> 'Our company has won several awards for environmental responsibility *which means that* our approach will always include sensitivity to green issues.'
>
> 'We have more than ten years' experience supplying senior computer staff to companies such as yours *which means that* we possess extensive knowledge of your staffing requirements.'

By spelling out relevant *company benefits* you also make it easier for new customers to risk making the changes involved in giving you their business.

As I shall explain in Stage Three, being able to initiate such a change in outlook and behaviour is central to selling success.

Put All Your Benefits to the Test

Not every benefit will be as relevant to a particular customer. The only way to ensure a close match between their needs and the benefits you have on offer is to subject each one to the 'So what?' test before including it in your sales presentation. Here's how it works.

> **Unique benefit**: 'Our new telephone switchboard is the simplest one on the market to learn and has built-in error checks.'
> 'So what?'
> **Relevant benefit**: 'With a company which is expanding as rapidly as yours, providing adequate training to receptionists could be a problem. Our switchboard cuts the training time to less than sixty seconds. What's more it prevents calls being misdirected, mistakes which could cost you new business or damage an existing relationship.'

> **Company benefit**: 'We are market leaders in developing accountancy software packages for small businesses.'
> 'So what?'
> **Relevant benefit**: 'Because our accountancy package can be used by any member of staff, you'll save yourself the overhead of a permanent bookkeeper or delays from using a part-timer. You'll reduce costs and still produce all your accounts accurately and on time.'

Remember the only benefits of relevance to most business customers are those which demonstrate how they can:

- increase profits;
- reduce overheads;
- improve return on investment;
- enhance cash flow.

Any other benefits come second – usually by a very long way.

Benefits and Buying

Having reviewed the different types of benefits, we should now consider how you can discover which benefits will be of greatest appeal to prospective customers so as to include them in your sales presentations. What these benefits are depends to a large extent on the nature of the business contemplated. There are three types of purchase.

- new buys;
- straight rebuys;
- modified rebuys.

New Buys

This involves presenting either to customers with whom you have done no previous business or to existing customers interested in buying a different line.

Straight Rebuys

You have already won their business and supplied them over a period. Now the contract is up for renewal or they need fresh supplies.

Straight rebuys usually involve less time and effort than new buys, but beware of complacency. While being an established and satisfactory supplier clearly improves your chances, success is by no means guaranteed.

Events over which you have no control can disrupt the closest business relationship. You could, for example, fall victim to office politics. A new buyer decides to demonstrate independence by changing suppliers.

A sales director may close down even a successful line due to changes in company policy. This happened to one major British gift manufacturer after the new marketing director of a large retail chain decided to stop selling fancy goods. He did so as part of his policy to bring the chain more upmarket, despite the fact that gift items were highly profitable.

This decision meant a loss of business for the gift manufacturer, who had been dealing successfully with that chain for more than twenty years, worth in excess of £250,000 annually.

Another frequent cause of lost business is unvoiced criticism of the service provided. Since they are never stated openly such complaints are impossible to correct or rebut. The first a supplier learns of them is when the business is lost. Unfortunately, as we shall see in Stage Five, the majority of complaints come into this category.

It is possible to safeguard yourself to some extent by developing contacts within the company to provide advance warning if anything starts going wrong.

Modified Rebuys

These occur whenever a customer wants changes in the nature of the goods or services supplied.

When building a relationship with new customers (Stage Five), it is important to ensure they are aware of *all* the benefits your company is able to offer.

Unless discouraged from doing so, buyers tend to rigidly pigeon-hole suppliers and so fail to appreciate their capacity for coping with changing demands.

The surest strategy is to pre-empt the modified rebuy by initiating changes yourself.

A company selling software might tell one of their customers: 'We know you have always bought this training package. But this latest upgrade offers so many powerful new features we felt sure you'd want advance information on it.'

Proposing a modified rebuy offers several important selling advantages.

- Your relationship with the key decision makers is strengthened. Recognising you have their best interests at heart encourages loyalty by making you 'part of their team'.
- You achieve a closer correspondence between your customers' needs and the benefits being provided. The better this match the greater will be their commitment to buying from you.

- The shared learning experience which occurs during a modified rebuy increases understanding between yourself and the customer, making it easier to handle any problems in the future.

The most effective way of determining the benefits most likely to appeal to customers, new or existing, is to change perspective and see your business through the eyes of a customer.

Ask: 'What benefits can we offer which are so exceptional the customer would be crazy to buy from a competitor?'

MAKING THE GRASS EVEN GREENER

For more than two decades ChemLawn, a $355 million a year Columbia, Ohio based company, practically owned the market in commercial lawn maintenance.

Then a few years ago smaller companies came into the picture placing ChemLawn under competitive pressure.

'For many years we simply told customers what we had to offer,' commented vice-president for sales David Malberger. 'Now we had to find out what they wanted.'

Their response was to convene an all-day conference of ChemLawn's largest customers. Seeing their business through the eyes of its customers ChemLawn found they were not seen as a total lawn care provider. This had caused established clients to turn to smaller firms for their other landscaping needs.

Responding to these comments ChemLawn quickly developed fresh sales presentations which won them valuable new contracts.

The result was to make the grass even greener by pushing sales up 20 per cent.

Lesson: See the world through your clients' eyes to ensure you are fully exploiting all the benefits your company can offer.

Often the full value of the benefits you can offer only becomes apparent after you have conducted careful research into your prospective customer's requirements. This topic will be dealt with in Stage Two.

ACTION PLAN 1

To get the best from this practical training book take the time to work with the action plans which can be found at the end of each chapter.

These enable you to gain the greatest benefit from the procedures described, while providing important insights into your own company's strengths.

Analysing your benefits

List all the features your company provides, then identify benefits using the phrase '. . . *which means that* . . .' Identify these benefits as standard (SB), double (DB), chained (CB), unique (UB) or company (CMB).

Action plan

Features of my business		*Benefit to customers*
. . . .	*which means that*	. . . .
. . . .	*which means that*	. . . .

.... *which means that* ....

.... *which means that* ....

.... *which means that* ....

.... *which means that* ....

.... *which means that* ....

.... *which means that* ....

.... *which means that* ....

.... *which means that* ....

Now take a unique benefit and build a chaining tree, keeping in mind a particular customer or type of customer for whom these benefits might have the greatest appeal.

KEY POINTS

- Before you can find new customers you must be clear about the exact nature of your business.
- Since people buy benefits and not features you must next identify the full range of these.
- Use the phrase '... which means that ...' to convert features into benefits.
- There are five types of benefit: standard, double, chained, unique and company. Double benefits have the greatest power to persuade and should always be included in the sales presentation.
- Ask: 'What benefits can my company offer which are so exceptional the customer would be crazy to buy from a competitor?'

- The benefits of greatest appeal to a particular customer vary according to the sort of purchase being made.
- Benefits must be matched to the exact requirements of the customer. These needs can only be identified by careful research (see Stage Two).

2 IN THE BEGINNING IS THE CUSTOMER

'THERE'S only one boss. And he can fire everybody in the company from the chairman down, by spending his money somewhere else.'

Sam Walton, founder of Wal-Mart

WHAT THAT all-powerful individual the late Sam Walton had in mind is, of course, your customer.

No product however ingenious, no service however advantageous has any commercial future unless somebody – preferably many somebodies – is prepared to buy it.

Customers are your reason for being in business and the only people who can keep you in business.

Unfortunately, while all customers might appear to be equally desirable and welcome, especially if you have just started out in business, this is not always the case.

As with the creatures in George Orwell's *Animal Farm,* some customers are more equal than others!

Enthusiastically making sales presentations to the wrong kind of customers can prove as damaging to commercial survival as failing to be single minded in your pursuit of new business.

Not only will you be squandering the precious and finite resources of time and money, but you will also be increasing the risk of damaging your reputation by producing dissatisfied customers.

Identifying the Right Customers – A Tale of Two Motorists

Imagine you own a garage in an area which has two distinct types of motorist.

One group is affluent young executives who drive expensive performance cars. They enjoy a high disposable income and set exacting standards when caring for their expensive cars. You know they maintain these vehicles in first-class condition, have them serviced regularly and expect to pay higher than average costs for specialist labour and spares.

The second group consists of family motorists, many with children, all with a lower disposable income. They drive production line cars which are not always regularly serviced. They watch every penny on the bill and demand the best possible value for money.

Which of these two groups of business would it prove most profitable to win?

While it may appear that the well-heeled executives would make the best customers this is not necessarily the case. For one thing, they are a group with few ties who are likely to be moved on by their firms at short notice.

This makes it impossible to ensure their loyalty, no matter how good the service you provide. At the same time employing specialist mechanics to service their performance vehicles and carrying stocks of costly spares will lead to high overheads. Any attempts on your part to save money by using less expert engineers or by ordering spares only as they are needed will result in a lower standard of service and dissatisfied customers.

In the long term you could find it far more profitable to direct your sales efforts to the less affluent but potentially loyal motorists from whom you are able to provide a superior service at a reasonable cost. Additional benefits from winning the business of these customers include:

- there are usually many more of them;
- having a family makes them less likely to relocate;
- as their children become teenagers and want cars of their own they are most likely to buy from a trusted supplier.

'Right' customers, therefore, are not necessarily those who provide the highest immediate profits or those who are easiest to attract.

Rather they are customers who are most likely to remain loyal, and for whom you are able to provide an exceptional service and genuine solutions.

Prospective customers who fail to satisfy these criteria are probably not worth encouraging.

While telling an eager prospect 'What we are selling is not right for you' may sound like commercial folly, it actually makes good commercial sense.

SAYING 'NO' SAFEGUARDS REPUTATIONS

Directors of Black Mountain Spring Water Company had the opportunity of expanding their business into a new region. They turned it down because it would not have been possible to offer the level of service their reputation demanded. A senior manager explained: 'To provide the kind of service we promised our customers, we had no other choice.'

Lesson: A successful company is one which never promises more than it can deliver.

Characteristics of Loyal Customers

Research shows that the customers most likely to remain loyal are those who:

- come via personal referral rather than through advertising;
- own their own homes;
- are middle aged;
- live in rural communities.

Heading the list of consumers least likely to remain loyal, no matter how pleased with your performance, are the migratory urban young whose business relationships are disrupted each time they move.

It is important to realise, however, that there is no such thing as inherently disloyal customers. As the American insurance giant USAA has shown (see below), consumers who are disloyal and unprofitable for one company may be loyal and profitable for another.

CREATING LOYALTY BY ENSURING CONTINUITY

The mobility of military officers makes them potentially disloyal customers. Yet this group provides core business for American car insurers USAA. By creating a centralised database and telephone sales system, USAA has turned itself into a loyalty leader with an astonishing 98 per cent retention rate.

Their system means that no matter where in the world they have been posted a customer can always talk to the same insurance agent.

This continuity ensures loyalty by allowing a friendly relationship to develop between client and agent.

It saves USAA the expense and trouble of having to transfer or create new records every time a client is posted, as well as the costs of replacing lost clients.

Lesson: Ingenuity in servicing customers others regard as disloyal can provide an excellent source of new business.

Your Customers and the 80/20 Rule

The classic pyramid model is based on the famous 80/20 rule devised by Italian economist Vilfredo Pareto. This states that 80 per cent of profits come from 20 per cent of their customer base.

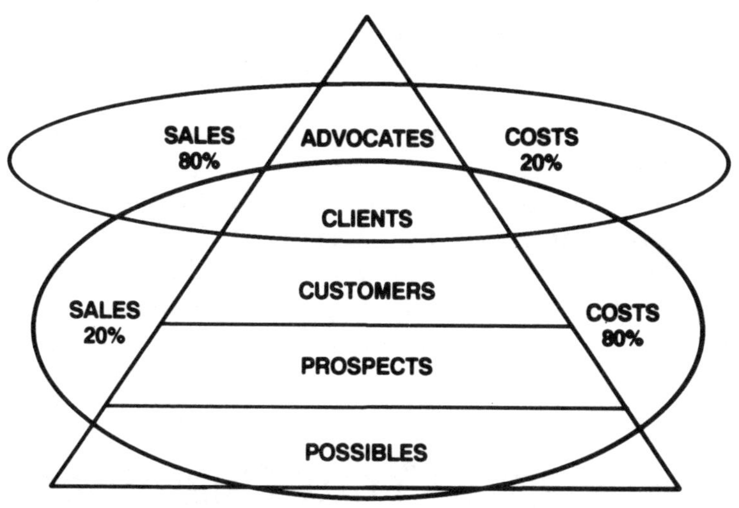

This structure reflects the loyalty ladder in which your total potential market is ranked in degrees of commitment to your company.

ADVOCATES	Recommend you to others
CLIENTS	Buy from you frequently
CUSTOMERS	Buy from you once
PROSPECTS	In the market and qualified to buy
POSSIBLES	In the market from time to time, but not necessarily qualified to buy

By qualified I mean that they have both a potential interest in your product and the authority to make purchases.

A computer manager is a qualified prospect for a software supply company. The office clerk, no matter how keen on computers, will probably be unqualified at that time. However he, or she, remains in the market as a 'possible', since promotion or some similar change in circumstances could qualify them to become prospects. It is always worthwhile cultivating ambitious youngsters in any company because, if you can win their loyalty at an early stage, they provide the longest lifetime spend.

As both the pyramid and the loyalty ladder show, the most profitable customers are also the fewest in number.

Beneath them, in increasing quantities, are medium and then low-volume customers, with prospects and possibles, who may or may not turn into prospects forming the base. The base comprises your entire market.

Descend down either the pyramid or ladder and you greatly expand the number of potential customers. At the same time reaching them becomes increasingly difficult and expensive.

Analysing Your Customer Base

Drawing up a list of potential new customers involves:

- analysing the profile of existing customers and
- identifying customers with similar characteristics.

For consumer products like food and drink, the process involves extensive research to come up with typical consumer profiles based on age, sex, socioeconomic grouping and certain lifestyle attributes.

Targeting the business market is normally conducted on the basis of industrial classification and occupational grouping. While this may simplify your research task, there are certain aspects of business marketing that can complicate the task. Unlike consumers, businesses rarely make purchase decisions on impulse or in isolation. Collective decision making is the rule rather than the exception, which may mean delays in making the sales. This is a problem I will be looking at in Stage Two.

One method of drawing up a list of potential new

customers is to analyse the characteristics of existing clients, scoring them for importance on a scale of, say, 1 – 10. Ways in which you can do this are explained in Action Plan 3 at the end of this chapter.

By examining the type of businesses they run in terms of size, turnover, product and/or service offered, location, decision-making procedures and so on, patterns emerge which offer clear indications of where you are most likely to find new business.

In the illustration overleaf seven such key characteristics have been identified by the letters A to G.

The table shows the scores allocated to each of these. On both graphs these scores have been plotted for an existing and profitable PROFILE using a continuous line.

On the left-hand graph the PROFILE client is compared with potential client A (dotted line). Since this client has very similar scores it is probable they will prove far more receptive to your sales presentation than Client B (dotted line, right-hand graph) which, as the plot clearly shows, differs significantly on these key characteristics.

By graphing them in this way similarities and differences become more readily apparent.

You may discover, for instance, that the majority of your core customers are small retailers or professional partnerships like solicitors and accountants.

Provided that the market is not saturated, it's a fair bet that similar needs exist for your products among companies with the same business profile.

If your analysis is performed correctly the resulting customer profile should be fairly homogeneous in regard to purchasing history, demographics, business profile and so on.

Apart from making it easier for you to offer an excellent service, such homogeneity significantly reduces your marketing expenses.

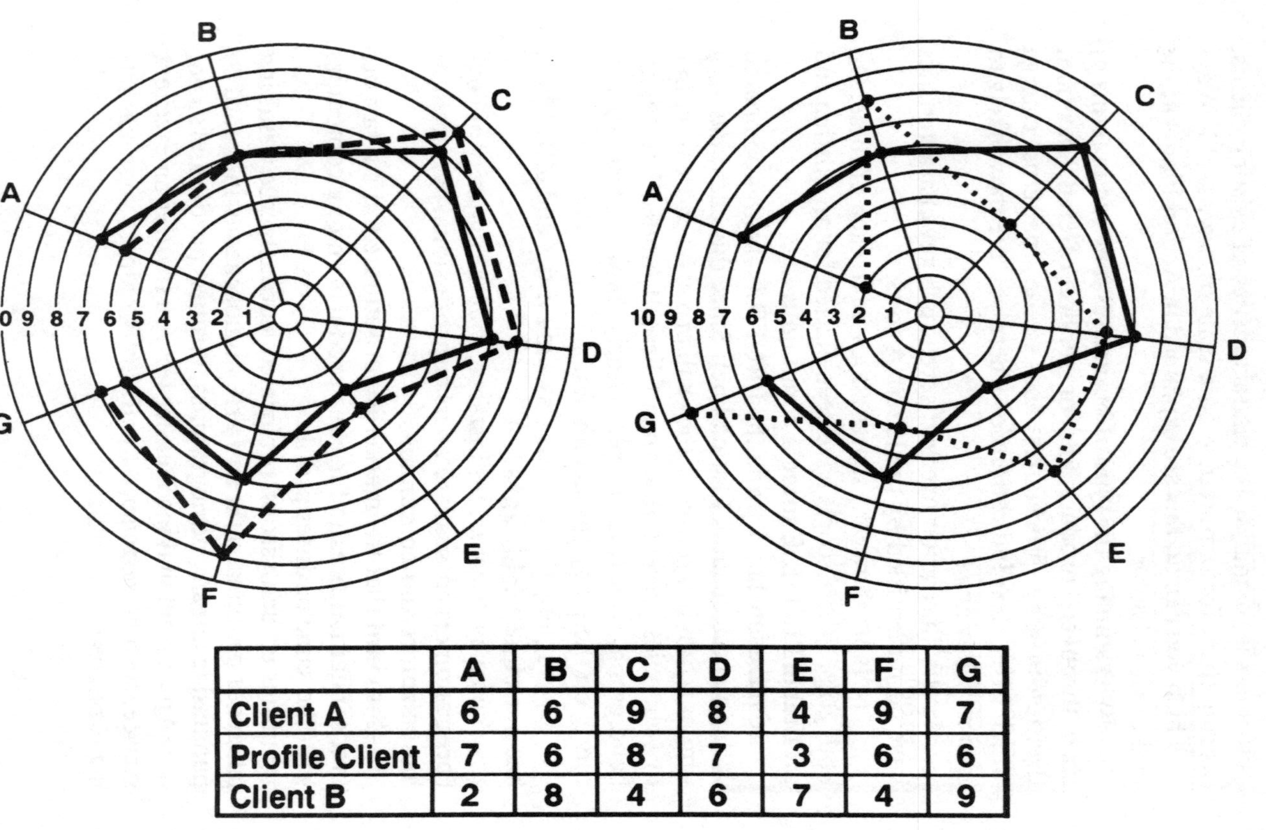

	A	B	C	D	E	F	G
Client A	6	6	9	8	4	9	7
Profile Client	7	6	8	7	3	6	6
Client B	2	8	4	6	7	4	9

THE GOSPEL ACCORDING TO AGA

David Ogilvy, chairman of the international advertising agency Ogilvy and Mather, started his career selling solid fuel cookers. Research showed him that the stoves sold particularly well among Scottish clergy. With the aid of a clerical directory he drew up a list of churchmen and visited each to proclaim the gospel according to Aga.

His strategy worked so well he quickly became the company's top salesperson.

Lesson: Good research is the basis of identifying new business.

Customers and Your Company's Maturity

There are marked similarities between the growth curves of companies, ecosystems and living organisms.

Both move from infancy into a period of rapid growth, level off at maturity, and decline into senility and extinction.

The crucial difference between companies and living organisms is that, through constant rejuvenation, businesses achieve a far greater lifespan. In theory, at least, a well-managed company should enjoy virtually everlasting life, although it will have to undergo continuous and radical change in order to do so.

The growth chart below illustrates the five possible levels of maturity of a company.

The comments overleaf will help you locate your own company's position on the chart.

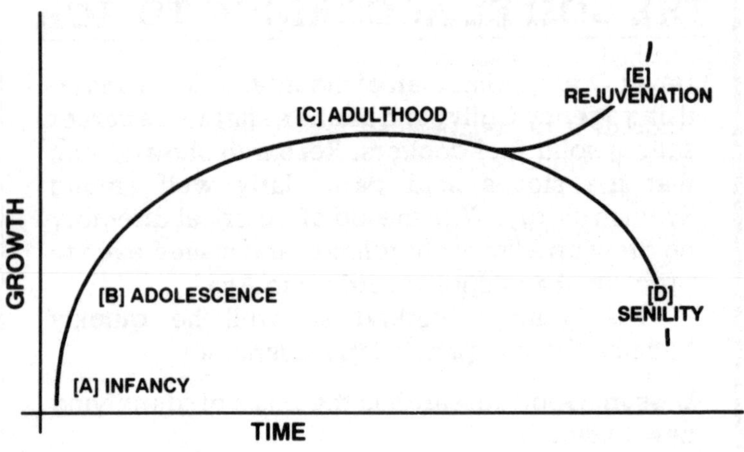

[**A**] *Infancy*: Start-ups and new ventures.
[**B**] *Adolescence*: The company experiences rapid growth.
[**C**] *Adulthood*: Growth slows as the company depends increasingly on the loyalty of established customers.
[**D**] *Senility*: The business is starting to die. Changes have to be made urgently if it is to survive.
[**E**] *Rejuvenation*: Instead of slipping into decline and extinction the company has been reborn by innovative marketing and other growth-enhancing strategies.

Which customers are 'right' for your business depends on the company's level of development.

Winning New Business at Infancy

The most pressing concern at this lowest level of maturity is to expand your customer base as rapidly as possible. This is often best achieved through networking, a process described in Chapter 3.

Where directors and/or managers have worked in the same line of business before, they may be able to make a significant contribution to such a network. But it is unwise to rely too heavily on such contacts. Even when previous contracts of employment allow such customers to be approached, they may be unwilling to change their existing suppliers.

Indeed, if the relationship between supplier and buyer has been developed effectively (see Stage Five), it may take a great deal to persuade them to change their allegiances.

Bear in mind also that in the rapidly changing world of business, even the best contacts quickly become useless as previous clients are promoted to other jobs, move to different companies, retire, are made redundant and so on.

While a rapid expansion of your cusomter base is essential, growth at infancy must be tempered with caution.

Apart from the risk of going after the wrong type of customers, as discussed above, pursuing too many 'right' prospects can also create problems serious enough to imperil your company's future.

Going for growth at any price may result in cash-flow problems, as well as difficulties with staffing, achieving deadlines, meeting output quotas and maintaining a consistently high quality.

Rapid growth also increases the risk of taking on financially dubious customers who, should they go down, may drag you with them.

When creating core customers keep these points in mind.

- Never be too eager to enter into major contracts with new customers. As well as checking their financial standing through a credit agency, make discreet enquiries among other suppliers to discover how promptly their accounts are settled. Simply because you are dealing with a large and wealthy company does not necessarily mean they pay creditors within thirty days. Taking on too many slow payers could cause you severe cash-flow problems.
- Avoid the temptation to win customers by undercutting

the competition. If you are able to offer lower costs through greater efficiencies, reduced overheads etc., without affecting quality, all well and good. But a price-cutting war based on wafer-thin margins, or even selling below cost price, is suicidal for any start-up. While you may attract a large volume of new business in a short space of time, customers for whom price is the only consideration are the ones least likely to remain loyal. When you are finally forced to raise prices they will desert you just as swiftly.

Competing on price alone also inhibits growth and makes it impossible to maintain high quality. As a result your reputation may be jeopardised to such an extent that it becomes far harder for your company to grow into the next level of development – adolescence.

Winning New Business in Adolescence

At this level of maturity your company has established a core of loyal customers and is continuing to win new business. The main dangers now are a desire to take things more easily or being tempted into expanding too rapidly.

Taking life too easily

This potentially fatal mistake is more likely to occur in small to medium-sized companies where the founders, having exhausted themselves launching their business into orbit, take what they regard as a well-deserved rest. The result is often a stalled ascent, followed by a rapid and sometimes catastrophic descent.

Only by striving constantly to find and win new business can you ensure continued growth and the replacement of customers who, for one reason or another, have become disloyal (see following).

Expanding too rapidly

Accelerated expansion during adolescence leads to a danger of company growth outpacing the ability of managers to stay in charge of events.

The entrepreneurial skills necessary for creating a new business are often unsuited to the challenge of moving from adolescence to adulthood. This happened at the birth of the computer industry, around 1977, when companies mushroomed in the bay area of San Francisco.

High-tech start-ups by enthusiasts, who remained hobbyists at heart, enjoyed phenomenal early growth, moving in a space of weeks from infancy to advanced adolescence.

Stephen Wozniak (Woz), co-founder of Apple Computers, recalls sales being made at such a rate that the drawers and cupboards in their garage factory were full of dollar bills they had not found time to pay into the bank. The shirt-sleeved founders of these start-ups were strong on electronic wizardry and idealism, but almost totally lacking in conventional management skills.

Apple, after some painful managerial shake-ups which saw the departure of both Woz and, later, his co-founder Stephen Jobs, went on to become a world leader. But many of the other start-ups which soared in the 1970s had sunk without trace within a decade.

Another hazard as adolescence gives way to adulthood is a lack of imagination when seeking out new business to win. This vision can become so blinkered that only one marketing goal is ever even considered.

Unfortunately, no matter how many safeguards you build into any business there will always be a danger that some unforeseeable circumstance can damage or even totally destroy your current line of business. Unless you have the flexibility and imagination to move swiftly should such a disaster occur, your company could go under.

STAGS AT BAY

A British company specialising in exporting breeding stags from Eastern Europe to American deer farmers saw their established and profitable business destroyed in a matter of weeks by the outbreak of BSE (bovine spongiform encephalopathy) among cattle. Although deer are not affected by BSE, buyers panicked in the face of massive publicity and refused further deliveries. They survived by rapidly diversifying away from breeding into the production of venison.

Lesson: Avoid putting all your eggs in one basket. You can never protect yourself against every eventuality.

Creativity when reviewing your range of benefits makes it far easier to rebuild a threatened business. But imaginative selling is not a skill which can be turned on or off at will. It only flourishes in company cultures which encourage flexible thinking as a routine management tool.

Even if business is booming, a lack of vision when reviewing benefits means lost sales.

I shall be considering this barrier to continued growth in Stage Two and offering practical suggestions to enhance creativity.

If your company is at the adolescent level watch for these seven points which can make or break you.

1. Keep a close watch on your margins. Always be aware of whether they are going up or down.
2. Never depend for the majority of your business on a small number of high-volume customers.
3. Pay more attention to orders than shipments. Never confuse orders with invoices or invoices with receipts.

4. Without sacrificing quality, become cost conscious and profit orientated. Do not be led astray by the gross. Place this motto above your desk and read it daily: 'Turnover is vanity – profit is sanity!'
5. Accept risks only when you are in a position to exert control over events. Never risk what you cannot afford to lose.
6. Constantly review your products or services to ensure the highest possible quality tailored to your customers' specific needs.
7. Always be on the look-out for ways of enhancing customer satisfaction.

Winning New Business in Adulthood

The worst blunder that can be committed by a company at this level of maturity is to start taking the loyalty of existing customers for granted. Customer satisfaction is not, unfortunately, any guarantee of customer retention.

Even companies offering an excellent service and high-quality products lose up to a quarter of their customer base each year, no matter how delighted those purchasers claim to be.

The motor industry, for example, consistently achieves satisfaction scores of 85 to 95 per cent from their customers, yet repurchase rates on a particular model average only 40 per cent!

In adulthood, a company has only three possible routes into the future.

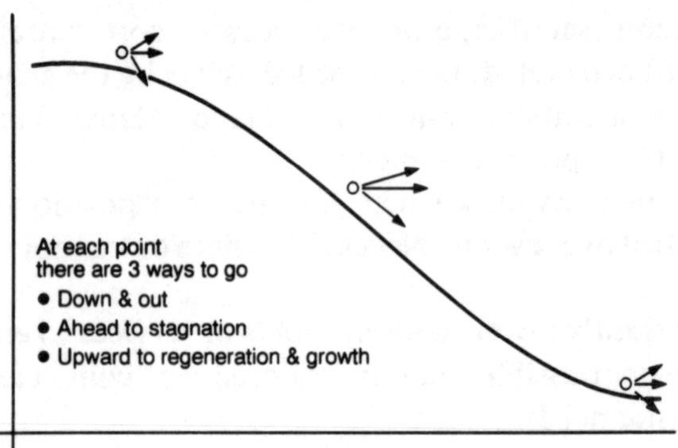

At each point
there are 3 ways to go
• Down & out
• Ahead to stagnation
• Upward to regeneration & growth

Over the top and downhill all the way

In a declining company customers are being lost faster than new business is being won. This may happen gradually over a period of months, even years, or catastrophically perhaps through the loss of a major account or fatally adverse publicity. In the first instance measures can often be taken to nurse an ailing organisation back to health. In the second there is a grave risk that the patient will haemorrhage to death before help arrives.

The following are among the most common reasons for losing previously loyal customers.

- Changes in senior management. New appointees typically like to distance themselves from the old regime by dismantling most of the systems created by their predecessors.
- Changes within your own organisation. Buyers prefer doing business with people they know. If key members of your sales or management team move elsewhere, some customers will inevitably follow them.

  As USAA showed, ensuring continuity between the customer and those who directly serve them is the key to retaining their loyalty. This can only happen if you regard your own staff as internal customers and work hard at keeping them loyal.
- Unresolved complaints erode customer loyalty. Research

suggests that only 3 per cent of customers who experience a problem complain directly to head office. The majority grumble, sulk and take their business elsewhere.

This is especially likely when the criticisms arise from the way in which a service has been delivered – the so-called 'process' dimension of selling.

One computer supplier lost business worth hundreds of thousands of pounds when a new receptionist treated the managing director of a major client in a way he considered 'discourteous'. Instead of voicing his anger openly the director simply dropped them from his list of suppliers.

- Customers cease trading. In smaller firms the retirement or death of the proprietor and disputes among family members may cause the company to close.

Other reasons for lost customers may include:

- bankruptcy;
- relocation;
- acquisition by another company with their own suppliers;
- ending a line which requires your product;
- prolonged industrial action;
- as with the BSE scare (see above) catastrophically bad publicity.
- fire, flood, earthquake and other natural disasters.

Apart from the last two reasons listed above, there is much you can do to prevent unnecessary lost of business through the process known as 'franchising' customers. I shall explain how this may be achieved in Stage Five.

Straight ahead to oblivion

While it is obviously vital to retain profitable accounts, following this path too wholeheartedly can prove commercially disastrous.

Because established customers tend to oppose changes in familiar products, the company's freedom to modify existing products, introduce new lines or raise prices in line with increased costs is restricted. This creates a classic marketing dilemma. Change a key product or service and you risk alienating your core customers.

Neglect such changes and margins will be eroded while the product line is increasingly seen as stale, tired and unexciting.

CLASSIC COKE – CLASSIC BLUNDER

In April 1985 Coca-Cola changed the formula of its flagship brand for the first time in ninety-nine years. 'The best has been made even better', claimed Coke's Chairperson Robert Goizueta.

Coke lovers, outraged by the sweeter taste, vehemently disagreed. Three months later the Real Thing was back on the shelves, renamed Classic Coke.

Within weeks it was outselling the new brand three to one. 'The passion for original Coke was something that just flat caught us by surprise,' admitted President Donald Keough.

Coca-Cola's size and their rapid response to public demand allowed the Atlanta-based company not only to survive but profit from the furore. Overall, Coca-Cola sales rose by 8 per cent that year. A less substantial company might have been fatally wounded by a similar marketing error.

Lesson: Changing a familiar brand carries with it the risk of alienating loyal consumers without attracting new ones in sufficient numbers to replace them.

Ever upwards – the regeneration curve

Many of the reasons why companies fail, such as inadequate credit control or managerial incompetence, lie outside the scope of this book.

The radical changes necessary to rescue stagnating companies from the consequences of their blindness and inertia can only be made by tough, visionary executives willing and able to accept that the business they move into may be very different from their traditional market place.

THE BIG BLUE BLUES

In 1992 IBM recorded a loss of $4.96 billion (£3.28 billion), the largest ever corporate deficit. Within two days the company's stock lost $6 billion in value and was dubbed the General Motors of high technology.

Why?

Some business analysts have charged both companies with missing generational changes in their markets, failing to take new competitors seriously and making only half-hearted attempts to change their ways. They claim the stumbling giant failed to adapt to a world of lean, nimble 'clone' makers.

Glenn Henry, former IBM man and now a senior vice-president at one of those clone makers, Dell, comments: 'If all you've done is herd elephants and you've never seen a rabbit, you can tell a fat elephant from a skinny one but you can't tell that it's 2 tons too heavy.'

Lesson: Avoid stagnation by seeking new business in unfamiliar terrain.

Listen to your customers and then develop new products or services based on their needs. At the same time, beware developing endless versions of the same basic products.

The only reason why people will purchase a 'new and improved' model is if it offers them the benefits of significant savings in time and/or cost.

Avoid the temptation of closing your eyes to signs of trouble, perhaps by taking refuge in the reassuring excuse that: 'The downturn is only a blip. It is an anomaly the market place will soon correct.'

Be alert for warning signs such as customers demanding lower prices or tougher terms before reordering, a slowdown in payments or delays in shipments.

When changing strategies, never take half-hearted measures. Firing your cleaners won't get you out of trouble.

On the other hand, offering attractive incentive bonuses to top sales staff so they feel even more motivated to win new business just might.

Four Barriers to Winning New Business

At all stages of your company's growth four main barriers can exist which will severely limit, or even preclude entirely, the ability to win new business.

Barrier One: The Myth of the Better Mousetrap

Ralph Waldo Emerson claimed that if you 'write a better book, preach a better sermon, or make a better mouse-trap ... the world will beat a path to your door.'

A few years ago one company did, indeed, design and market the best mousetrap ever invented. It was a Rolls-Royce among mousetraps, much admired by all those involved in the business of trapping rodents. Sadly this world-beating mousetrap is no longer available. The company manufacturing it went bust!

While it is true that a few products or services really do have no rivals, these are rare exceptions.

The vast majority of the goods and services are derivative, 'me too' products with a few added benefits to provide a *unique selling point* (USP).

One of the very few exceptions to this rule was the drilling bit used by oil companies and patented by Howard Hughes Snr. The basis of his family's billions, this bit was so special that when asked whether oil companies had any alternative but to use his bit, Howard Hughes replied sardonically: 'They could always try using a bucket and spade!'

In most cases, however, there are always competitors with alternatives which, even if inferior, capture a greater share of the market as a result of more successful selling.

Golden rule: Be proactive in winning new business. Wait for your customers to come calling and bailiffs not buyers will be beating a path to your door!

Barrier Two: A Reluctance to Confront Change

Large companies with bureaucratic cultures are more likely to speed down this road to disaster than smaller, flexible, organisations.

Psychosclerosis or 'hardening of the categories', a phrase coined by anthropologist Ashley Montagu, well describes the thinking found in companies which value tradition more highly than innovation.

Even twenty years ago, when the pace of change was far slower, the consequences of failing to move with the times was not always critical. Today it is inevitably fatal.

Tom Peters, co-author of *In Search of Excellence*, recalls

that a few decades ago, while he was working at McKinsey and Co., there was no need to consider inflation when making cash-flow projections for quarter of a billion dollar petrochemical facilities. They believed supply, demand and commodity prices could all be predicted with a fine degree of accuracy over a twenty-year period.

Peters now believes that 'if you aren't reorganising pretty substantially once every six to twelve months, you're probably out of step with the times.'

A culture of constant change is vital for commercial success because other firms are changing all the time.

Between the start and end of today, for example, Toyota will have implemented another twenty changes in their manufacturing procedures, the majority suggested by production line workers.

Golden rule: Make change the only constant in your business life.

Barrier Three: Selling Snobbery

Selling is not only the world's oldest profession, but it is also the force behind all social progress. Nothing happens until something has been sold. (I know that another profession often claims this title. But it's only a subdivision of selling!)

Every product, service, friendship, marriage and even babies only started after one person sold something to somebody else!

A sale is the start of everything.

Unfortunately, many in business seem to consider selling as being beneath them. They regard it as somehow seedy and unprofessional, a career of dubious morality followed only by those fitted for nothing better.

Such attitudes not only represent the most misinformed and misguided form of snobbery, they are also commercial suicide.

It is only possible to make the powerful sales presentations needed to win new business against tough competition when you sell your products or services with confidence and pride.

Even subconscious doubts make it impossible to sell persuasively. After all, if you seem unconvinced and uncomfortable, think how your customer must be feeling!

To succeed with a sales presentation you must honestly, truly and deeply believe the benefits you can provide that customer are in their own best interests.

If you are unable to feel this way about selling, the only advice I can offer is to find another job.

I repeat: to win new business you must have the same level of faith in the value of your product that allowed the saints to go singing cheerfully to their martyrdom.

However, even when you believe wholeheartedly in what you are selling, doubts can still arise to undermine your self-confidence.

These misgivings are focused not on the merits of what is being sold, but on your own abilities. A key cause of anxiety and self-doubt is the fear of rejection. This can lead to a subconscious contempt for selling via a psychological process termed projection. It works like this. Negative feelings about yourself are projected on to the activity you are attempting, making it appear unworthy.

This makes you incapable of communicating the kind of assurance and energy essential when making sales in a highly competitive market place.

At the same time, failure to sell can be excused by the thought: 'What I attempted was beneath my dignity in the first place, so it's probably all for the best that I never succeeded!'

I shall be discussing these difficulties in more detail in Stage Four, when we consider how to make confident and powerful sales presentations. I will also be describing practical procedures for building confidence and controlling fears of rejection when selling.

Golden rule: Be proud of selling and constantly improve your presentational skills.

Barrier Four: Running with the Herd

Once upon a time an old farmer, living in the American south, started to sell fresh fruit from a roadside stall. Because his prices were low and the fruit of excellent quality, his business flourished. He opened more stalls and started advertising his produce. Before long people were driving miles to buy his fruit.

Being so busy with his business, the old man never found time to read the newspapers, watch television or even listen to the radio.

One day his nephew, a lecturer in economics, came on a visit and was horrified at the way his uncle was running the business. 'Don't you know the country is in deep recession?' he demanded. 'The only way you'll survive is by putting up prices and cutting down overheads. Stop advertising immediately and buy cheaper fruit.'

Concerned, the old man raised his prices, stocked his stalls with lower quality fruit and stopped advertising. His business slumped. Profit turned to loss. Finally he went bankrupt.

'My nephew was right,' the old man reflected sadly. 'I must have been crazy to think I could succeed in a recession!'

Many businesspeople appear to think along the same lines as that old farmer. Captivated by siren songs of impending doom they stop trying to win new business and quickly fall victim to the Law of Negative Thinking. Here are four golden rules for protecting yourself against self-defeating thinking.

- Stop being swayed by nay sayers and doom laden headlines.

  Press stories often reflect isolated incidents chosen for their sensational news value rather than trends relevant to your particular line of business.
- Avoid negative people, those emotional black holes who can quickly suck you dry of hope and ambition.
- Instead surround yourself with realistic optimists and

resilient winners. The fastest and surest way to become successful yourself is by helping other people, staff, colleagues and customers to be successes themselves.

- Take positive steps to win new business and your success will grow.

ACTION PLAN 2

Address your mind to these questions.

1. Are you running any of the risks or missing any of the opportunities described above for a company at your level of maturity?

2. Are you seeking the right customers, namely those most likely to prove loyal and profitable? Or have you fallen into the trap of chasing turnover rather than profit? Gear your business for the long haul rather than the quick fix.

3. Is your customer base homogeneous?

Shared characteristics make it easier to provide customers with a superior service and more likely that they will remain loyal.

4. Is your company expanding rapidly? Then review your customer base. Are you sure all your customers should continue being supplied on their current terms?

Profile them in terms of demographics, turnover, age, purchasing history and whatever other characteristics may be relevant.

If the 20/80 rule applies, prune your customer base to get rid of any who consume resource without making adequate return. But when making this calculation be sure to take account of the potential lifetime spend of such customers.

ACTION PLAN 3

Research potential customers to identify their standing on each of the features which characterise those providing you with the most profitable custom. The closer the match, the more likely it is you will be able to win their business, provide an excellent service and retain their loyalty.

Use the outline on page 48 to profile one or two of your most profitable and loyal customers.

Step One: Write key characteristics of such customers around the circumference of the circle. These are aspects of the business relationship you consider most relevant to its success. They might include: being on close terms with key decision makers, possessing specialist knowledge, the size of their organisation, their corporate cultures, and so on.

There is no point in including obvious points. If, for example, the only thing you manufacture are widgets the fact that your customer buys widgets is irrelevant since it is bound to be a characteristic shared by *all* those with whom you do business.

Focus on those aspects of the relationship which make it so special and mutually rewarding.

Step Two: Rate each of these factors in terms of its current importance. I suggest using a scale of 1 – 10. Factors you regard as especially significant might rate, say, 9 or 10 while those which are important but less crucial receive lower ratings. For instance, the fact that a personal contact enabled you to win the business in the first place might well become less significant once you had proved to be a reliable supplier.

Having scored this customer on each of the key factors, join the points to produce a profile.

Step Three: Research any potential customers to discover the extent to which those same characteristics apply.

Companies which best match your profiled customers will, in most cases, prove the most receptive and profitable.

This technique also makes it easier to identify any areas where further research needs to be done prior to the presentation.

KEY POINTS

- Be selective when finding customers. Invest the time, energy and costs involved in sales presentations only in those most likely to remain loyal and for whom you can offer a superb service.
- Have the courage to turn down business if unable to offer such a service. It makes sound commercial sense.
- But there is no such thing as an inherently disloyal customer. Those unprofitable to one company may prove a gold-mine for another.
- Identify new business opportunities by profiling current customers. Remember the 80/20 rule which states that 80 per cent of a company's business comes from just 20 per cent of its customers.
- The 'right' customers depend on your company's maturity. By seeking the appropriate new business at different levels of growth, you can experience continued expansion and rejuvenation rather than stagnation and demise.
- Always remain flexible in your sales strategy. Make creative thinking a routine management tool.

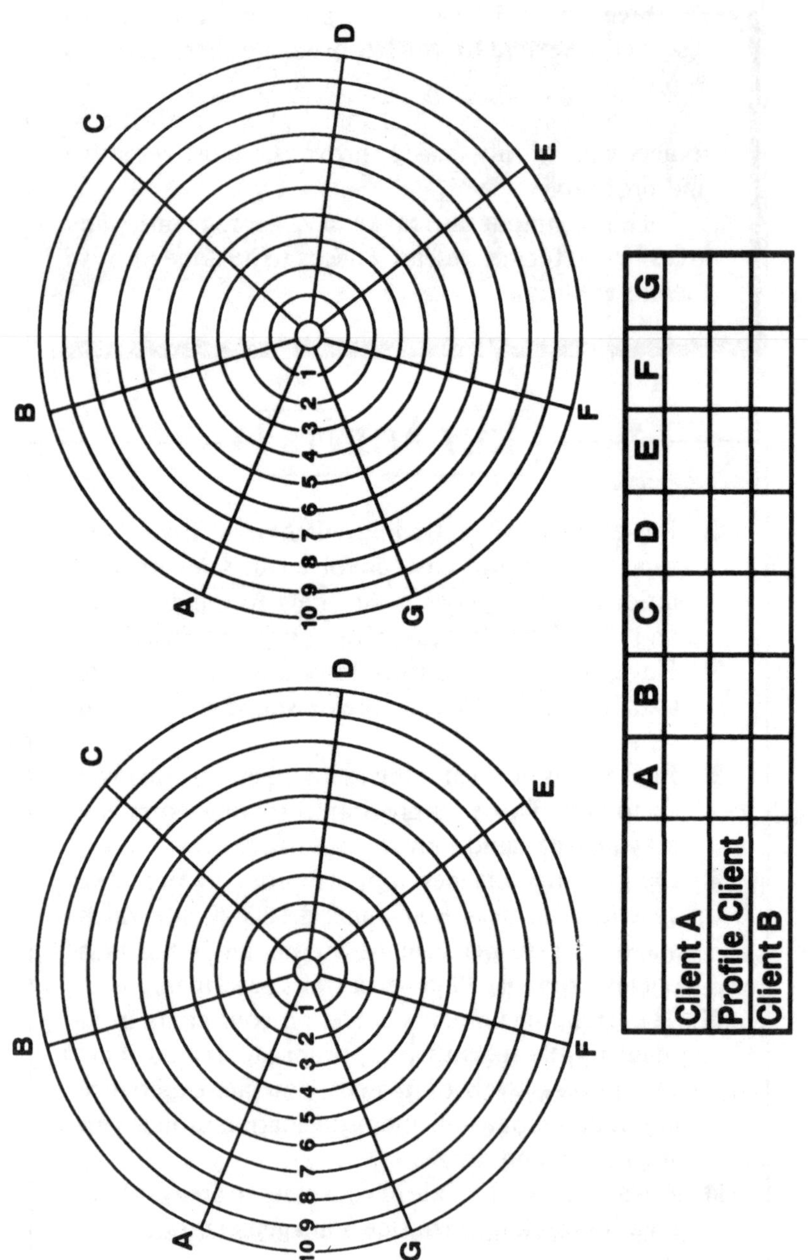

	A	B	C	D	E	F	G
Client A							
Profile Client							
Client B							

FINDING YOUR CUSTOMERS

WARNING – Customers Are Perishable!
Store sign

THAT STORE SIGN IS TRUE!
These days more than ever, customers have a sell-by date.

This is why, as I explained in the last chapter, business success demands that you constantly find new customers both to replace those who have perished and to enable your company to expand.

At this point in the book you should have a clear idea of what your company is actually selling – the benefits.

You should also be able to identify the type of customers likely to prove 'right' for your company at your level of maturity.

All that remains now is to find those customers, which is rather like saying, having established base camp at the foot of

Mount Everest, all we have to do now is climb the damn thing!

Like climbing a mountain, finding new customers involves not just skill, but stamina, persistence and a strong will to win.

What must constantly drive you onward is the goal of creating an even more prosperous and successful company; one that is determined to become the market leader in its particular field.

For, as a philosophical husky once commented: 'Until you get to be pack leader your view doesn't alter all that much!'

Here are your six most valuable sources in the quest for those new customers.

1. Directories

Reference works of the type which allowed David Ogilvy to find his clerical customers when preaching his gospel according to Aga (see page 29) are an invaluable source of leads. Almost every trade and profession has its own directories, listing names, addresses and corporate details on thousands of companies.

Trade associations can also be helpful, since many hold publicly available details on their members.

Do not overlook the most widely available of all directories, namely those published by the telephone companies. Especially useful are business listings, *Yellow Pages* and local directories. These contain millions of names and addresses conveniently sorted into industrial sectors. *Yellow Pages*, now also available on computer, can easily be accessed from any PC. Searching electronically significantly reduces the time taken to find suitable prospects and offers national coverage for the cost of a phone call.

For more selective business lists which provide individual names as well as addresses, you might consider approaching a specialist list broker who can sell you an updated database of potential customers. *Benns Direct Marketing Services Directory*, published twice a year, has details of such lists, or you could contact the British List Brokers Association who can send you information on its members.

2. Newspapers and Magazines

To the experienced eye, the pages of business press and quality newspapers offer a gold-mine of potential leads.

As well as printing details of recently awarded contracts, which could signal the need for new suppliers, these journals list major new appointments in the world of business and finance. Since it is common for newly-recruited directors to review their existing arrangements with company suppliers, this information could also provide useful openings. Early warning of a 'new broom' about to take up office presents an ideal opportunity to make your bid.

But beware, the technique of chasing promotions and appointments is a well-trodden path, so you'll have to make sure your approach is sufficiently arresting to stand out from the crowd.

Reading the business sections of the national newspapers can reap other rewards. It brings you up to date with the industry issues and rumours which affect the trading environment of your target company. A little knowledge of what's buzzing in your prospect's industry will go a long way towards making you sound knowledgeable and authoritative.

Indeed, newspaper articles quoting company spokes-people on the problems facing their industry or company is virtually an open tender to pitch. The public relations industry, for one, regularly scans the business press in search of the corporation under siege. If you do not already do so, start a cuttings library with relevant articles and news items filed under different headings. Consider, too, the advantages of subscribing to a news database, such as FT-Profile or Nexus. In addition to keeping you up to date with the latest trends and changes throughout industry and commerce, they help you discover all you can about a potential customer easily, rapidly and thoroughly when doing your preliminary research (see Stage Two).

3. Telemarketing

Knowing what makes your customers tick is one of the fundamental principles of good marketing.

And it makes a lot of sense when you are after more orders from existing customers.

But success in generating repeat business does depend on a good database which can be manipulated to group customers together by the type of product they bought, their address, age, sex and so on.

If you do not already have that kind of information on your customers, consider using the phone as one way of obtaining it. Carefully employed outbound telemarketing to customers you are already supplying can produce some startling results.

For example, when the Automobile Association directed a telemarketing campaign at members who had not renewed despite two requests to do so, 65 per cent of their calls proved successful.

HOW CHARRINGTONS HOTTED UP COAL SALES

When the solid fuel company Charringtons studied their customer database it revealed that some 30 per cent of customers had not placed an order for twelve months. A carefully constructed telemarketing campaign was devised and each dormant customer called.

Information was gathered on purchasing patterns, including reasons for not buying, and at the same time customers were offered seasonal price discounts.

As well as updating the database with valuable information, order sizes were increased by 27 per cent.

Lesson: Never neglect the telephone as a prime tool for generating new business.

If the appearance of a product is important, use pictures or diagrams to enhance your sales presentation.

EXPLOITING PICTURE POWER

After telemarketing attempts failed due to language difficulties, European Electronic, a company supplying high-speed printers and other components to mainframe users around the world, faxed product details to ten of the top Eastern European government departments.

The result was an immediate 70 per cent response rate and they took their first large order within 30 days.

Lesson: Remember the fax can help you exploit the persuasive power of pictures.

4. Old Friends

Asking friends or colleagues for custom can be tricky.

They may feel embarrassed by such overtures, either because they're not in a position to buy or out of fear of the 'friend's wedding photography' syndrome. Ask any photographer whether they would take pictures at a friend's wedding and the reply is usually a firm 'No!'

The risk of cutting off the bride's head or forgetting to load a film are sufficient to make sensible people hesitate before jeopardising a friendship.

Most of us harbour the guilt of fouling up a job for a friend or selling something to a colleague which subsequently breaks down.

Despite this, friends can be a useful source of new business, since they are probably as keen as you for your business to succeed, provided you approach them tactfully.

Explain exactly what will be involved and describe your ambitions for the business. Then let them approach you with a proposition.

If you do win their business, make doubly sure you always provide the highest possible standard.

5. Networking

As well as exploiting the principles of targeting, David Ogilvy's Aga sales strategy embraced another highly productive technique for finding new business – networking.

By meeting as many potential customers as possible, he was able to build up a network of goodwill ambassadors for his business.

Regardless of whether or not they made a purchase, the clergymen he had seen became an excellent source of recommendations.

Everyone likes to demonstrate a certain amount of knowledge and resourcefulness to friends and colleagues, and recommending a superior supplier makes them feel good.

There is nothing mystical or complex about networking – it just takes a little cheek, a lot of time, a strong constitution and great deal of positive listening (see Stage Two) and social chit-chat.

The aim of networking is to place yourself in as many situations as possible where you can talk about your business and learn about others. It's all about using your eyes and ears, and, where appropriate, your mouth. We've all heard about the legendary golf course transaction where deals are closed between strokes and lucrative contacts made at the nineteenth hole.

While it is unlikely you'll convert a total stranger into a customer with a few convivial words over a round of golf, you may well find yourself on a pitch list or be referred to another source of business.

The following list on network opportunities is not exhaustive, but should provide a starting point for your endeavours.

- sports clubs
- rotary clubs and chambers of commerce
- trade associations
- conference speaking
- exhibitions
- dinner parties
- charitable work
- interviewing staff.

The fundamental rule of business networking is to avoid the hard sell. Your networking career will be short-lived if you earn a reputation as a cheque-book chaser.

The best ploy is to ask questions which help you build up a picture of your new contact's business. As we shall see in Chapter 4, the more you know about your quarry, the more likely you are to find the right benefits to attract them to your sales proposal.

When the conversation comes round to what you do for

a living, talk about the work you do for other clients rather than what you could do for them.

A conversation along the lines of: 'We've recently installed new computers at Acme Inc. to speed up their processing of sales orders. The contract was worth over £2 million, but they reckon it will pay for itself within three years. . . '.

This is far more persuasive than: 'Isn't it about time you reviewed your computer systems – perhaps I could come and talk to you about it next week?'

The seasoned networker seizes every opportunity to meet potential clients and is never without business cards. I remember once, in the Hyatt Regency's rooftop swimming pool, high above Hong Kong harbour, chatting to a Japanese swimmer as we sat with our feet dangling in the water. The talk turned to business and he mentioned a new product which I felt my company might well be interested in buying. Without a flicker of emotion, my companion reached inside the pocket of his trunks and produced a fully waterproofed business card. At that point I became convinced that the Japanese are truly masters of selling.

There is, of course, an etiquette for the exchange of business cards.

Always ask for the other person's card first as this appears less pushy and is an open recognition of your interest. If your contact doesn't have a card, offer to write their details on the back of one of yours. This gives you an excuse to reach for your cards and, of course, enables you to capture that important information.

One businessman whose business prospered as a result of effective networking is Nick Smith, a partner in Smith & Watson Productions, a new and successful broadcast and corporate, film and video production company. 'Whoever you know is a potential contact who knows somebody else,' he says. 'If that person remembers you and is impressed by you, something may come out of it.'

He remembers, 'The biggest break we ever had – the

sort people dream of – came from a simple village fête down in Cornwall.

'My partner Chris Watson got chatting to the local MP, Liberal Democrat Matthew Taylor, who said he'd been put in charge of media handling for the party. He needed to try to find somebody to sort out the party political broadcasts which were dire, boring as hell and costing them a huge amount of money. Chris told him we could do it – really well – for half that sum.

'About six months later, Matthew Taylor came back to us wanting some suggestions. We wrote up what we wanted to do – and have been doing it for two years now. It's been a very successful campaign.

'The Liberal Democrats are probably the highest profile client we've got and that reassures other potential clients. What's been successful for us is that we never openly pitch to anybody.'

Your best sources of leads when networking are your established customers who know and trust you.

6. Networking Via Existing Customers

It may have become a sales cliché, but it is definitely easier to sell to someone who has already bought from you. And it is a good deal less expensive to make such sales. Existing customers already know you and your products; you already understand what they want and how much they are prepared to pay for it. You have a relationship.

The question is how you can retain that relationship and exploit it even further.

The importance of generating new business via existing customers cannot be emphasised too strongly. Satisfied customers are one of the most powerful marketing tools available to you. They are the foundations on which some of the world's mightiest business empires have been built.

BANKING ON WORD-OF-MOUTH SUCCESS

Midland Bank's twenty-four-hour telephone banking service, First Direct, illustrates the power of personal recommendation.

Over 28 per cent of their customers join on the recommendation of an existing customer – a far better performance than either press or TV advertising.

Lesson: Turn customers into goodwill ambassadors and your business will soar.

First, they offer the most persuasive of all advertisements, third-party endorsement. When sufficiently impressed by the service they received, customers are happy to start selling for you among their friends and colleagues.

Secondly, they are usually in the best position to know which other companies are most likely to be interested in buying from you.

Finally there is the added bonus that this sincere and enthusiastic sales force work for free! This is one reason why converting these leads from prospects to purchasers is highly cost effective.

Exploiting the Law of Multiple Effect

Assume that a satisfied customer is able to supply you with four leads – in my experience a fairly conservative estimate.

Also assume, again conservatively, that you win new business from three of these. Simple arithmetic reveals stunning sales growth achieved after only a few selling cycles.

If, for instance, you repeat the sales process six times your customer base will rise from two to over a thousand!

Here's what just one small part of a network of clients looks like after just six cycles. See page 60 for the actual numbers in growth of customers per cycle.

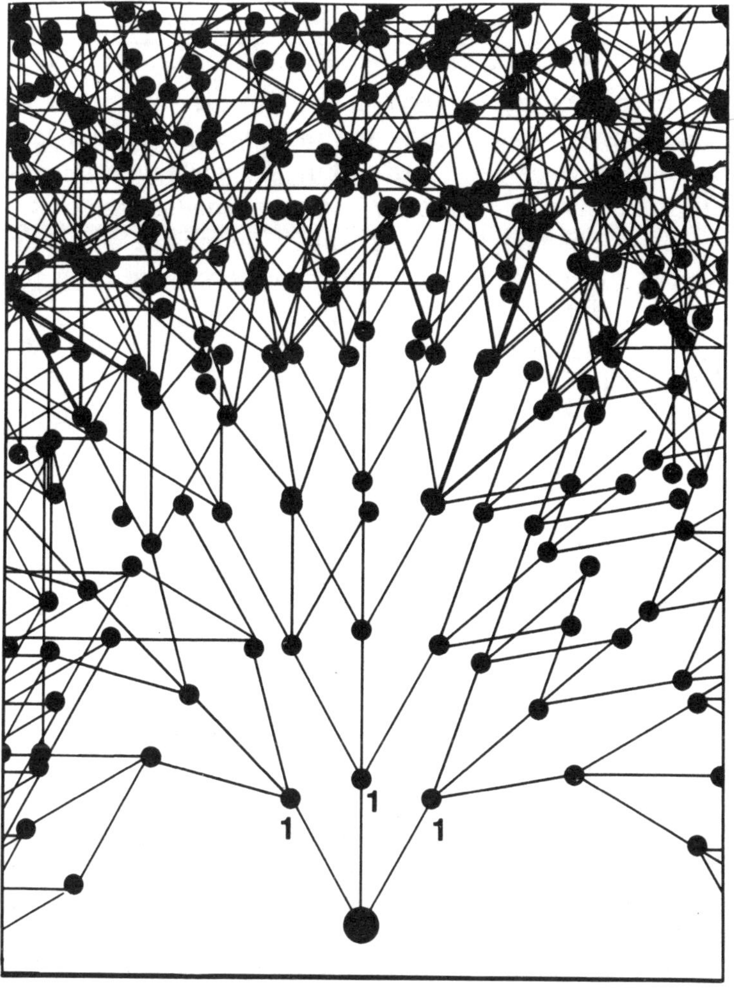

Cycle	Growth of customers per cycle
1	1 × 3 = 3
2	3 × 3 = 9
3	3 × 9 = 27
4	3 × 27 = 81
5	3 × 81 = 243
6	3 × 243 = 729
Grand total of customers = 1,092	

Even allowing for the fact that not every customer will provide new business leads and that even the hottest leads cannot always be persuaded to buy, networking in this way will still ensure your sales performance remains high.

Your company's culture will be optimistic, active and achieving as the result of positive energy created through a process I term the Law of Multiple Effects.

This might equally be called the Acorn Law since it states that to win big you can start small, provided you create the conditions necessary for rapid growth. The Law of Multiple Effects applies to every aspect of human behaviour from how we feel to the way we do business.

Success Creates Greater Success

Successful companies are characterised by an optimistic and confident corporate culture.

You know they are winners from the first moment of contact. Telephones are answered promptly and courteously. Car parks are well laid out and free from litter. Reception areas are clean and bright. Your greeting is friendly and informed.

Because employees see themselves as a team of achievers,

morale is high with staff working hard and efficiently. When the word gets around that this is a winning company, good people are eager to join and share their success. Customers are impressed by the willingness to do business and grateful to be served by such a pleasant and go-ahead firm.

Here the Law of Multiple Effects creates spirals of positive performance, each feeding on the last to generate a high level of commercial, and personal, achievement.

The constant supply of new leads from satisfied customers ensures that, even though some inevitably fail to produce immediate sales, high levels of energy and excitement are maintained within the company.

Unfortunately the Law of Multiple Effects also operates in reverse. When things start to slide, it can hasten the process of a company demise.

Failure Produces Further Failure

Just as a winning company communicates success in a host of different ways, failing firms also send unmistakable messages of falling morale.

Employees who lack confidence and are anxious about job security perform inefficiently.

There is a prevailing mood of 'What does it matter?' and 'Who gives a damn!', which swiftly destroys enthusiasm among newly recruited staff. Ambitious employees abandon ship leaving behind an increasingly demoralised workforce. Customers are unwilling to do business with such an unfriendly and ineffective organisation. Here the Law of Multiple Effects creates spirals of negative performance.

Following Up Leads

Having made contact it is essential to respond promptly to that opportunity for new business.

Research shows that leads followed up within a week have an 85 per cent chance of conversion. After two weeks your conversion rate drops to half. If you leave it for a month, you'll have a less than a one in five chance of closing that deal.

Always follow up every contact promptly and efficiently, so as not to miss that new customer's sell-by date.

ACTION PLAN 4

Using the form overleaf write down three possible sources of new business which are relevant to your business.

Now create a practical strategy for exploiting each of these.

Note:

- what action is to be taken to follow that lead;
- who is going to do it;
- when it is to be done. Setting a deadline is very important to achieving results.

After each action has been taken note down what happened. Do not feel discouraged by rejection or failure. Success in selling comes to those who are both well prepared and persistent. Never focus on setbacks. Instead, look at anything positive which came from this exercise, even if it was not finding a single, prospective customer. Did you obtain further leads?

Have you discovered ways in which your technique might be improved?

Are some of those sources unhelpful so far as your business is concerned?

There are always lessons to be learned from everything one does when selling. A failure often teaches a more important, albeit more painful, lesson than success.

Finding New Customers – Action Forms

SOURCE 1:

ACTION TO BE TAKEN:

BY:

DATE TO BE COMPLETED:

OUTCOME:

SOURCE 2:

ACTION TO BE TAKEN:

BY:

DATE TO BE COMPLETED:

OUTCOME:

SOURCE 3:

ACTION TO BE TAKEN:

BY:

DATE TO BE COMPLETED:

OUTCOME:

KEY POINTS

- There are six main sources for new customers:
  - directories
  - newspapers and magazines
  - telemarketing
  - friends
  - networking
  - existing customers.
- Word-of-mouth recommendation is your most powerful sales tool.
- Create a climate of success in your company so as to benefit from the positive spiral created by the Law of Multiple Effects.

STAGE TWO

Identifying and Meeting Your Customers' Needs

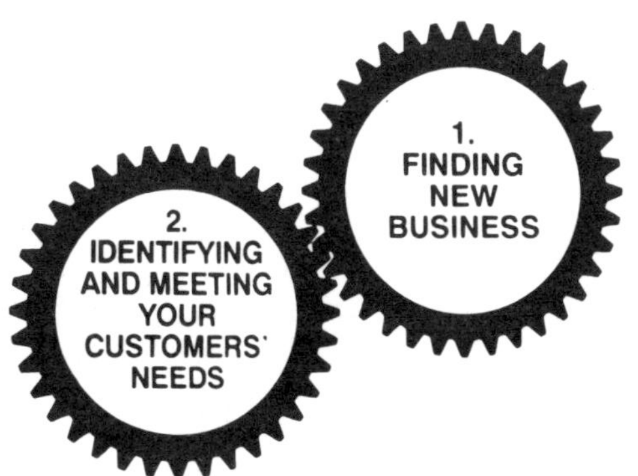

'CONSUMERS are statistics. Customers are people.'

Stanley Marcus, Chairman Emeritus, Neiman-Marcus

'TALKING to the salespeople on the floor, I would find out how our product was selling compared with the competition. Then I would ask what sort of problems they were having selling our merchandise. I wanted to have solutions to those problems *before* they were brought up in my meetings with the buyer or store owner.'

Victor 'I bought the company' Kiam, Going For It

GETTING INSIDE YOUR CUSTOMER'S HEAD

'WHEN you dance with your customer, let him lead!'

Anonymous

THE SECRET of winning new business can be summed up in three words – research, research, research.

To sell successfully and consistently your knowledge must be broad as well as deep, both general and specific.

As a background to any high level sales presentation you must possess a handful of general knowledge.

- **Business knowledge**: You must be well informed about the commercial climate at home and overseas.
- **Industry knowledge**: You should possess up-to-date information about your competitors' products, prices and positioning.

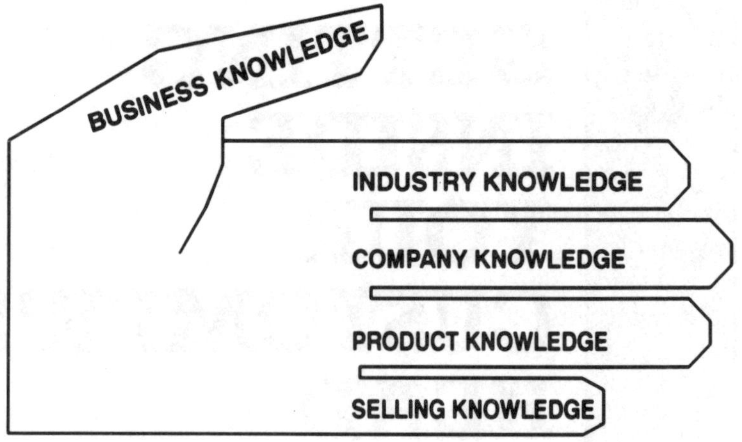

- **Company knowledge**: As ambassadors for their companies all sales personnel need to be well informed on company policy, schedules, marketing and advertising.
- **Product knowledge**: While this might appear obvious it is astonishing how many salespeople appear woefully ignorant of their products.
- **Selling knowledge**: Even experienced salespeople run the risk of getting trapped in their 'comfort zone' when selling and fail to update their sales skills.

Research suggests that the average sales professional actually sells for less than two hours a day, rarely making the first sales call until 11 o'clock in the morning. Just one in ten of sales people make more than five sales calls a day. A study at Columbia University in the USA showed that while 80 per cent of sales are closed at the fifth attempt, 48 per cent of all calls ended without even one shot at closing the deal.

The good news is that the idleness of many sales professionals provides great opportunities for those willing and able to chase new business enthusiastically, energetically and expertly.

As well as general knowledge it is essential to possess detailed information about prospective new customers.

'Doing your homework is probably the single most important part of any sales presentation,' says Graham Lancaster, chairman of Biss Lancaster PLC, one of Britain's top twenty PR companies, and author of *The 20 Per Cent Factor* (Kogan Page, 1993).

'If people invite you to present they've already accepted that you're competent at your craft skills and can do a reasonable job. What makes the crucial difference between success and failure is your knowledge of their sector, their positioning within that sector and the market dynamics of the industry they're in.

'All clients think their sector is very different to any other and they want some recognition of that understanding played back to them. You'll never succeed with a sales presentation you've done ten times before. Each one has to be tailor-made for a particular client.'

HOW ONE CLIENT ENJOYED FOOD FOR THOUGHT

When pitching for Capital Radio's business, PR consultancy John Cousins decided to record a special radio commercial. Their problem was to make sure Capital's newly-appointed managing director Richard Eyres would listen.

With the help of a former secretary they researched Eyres's personal interests. Armed with this knowledge they produced an entertaining commercial with an actor impersonating the station's top DJs.

Among the inside information the secretary recounted was Eyres's love for Danish pastries. That gave them the idea of sending him the tape plus some pastries. Unfortunately, those sold over-the-counter were too big to fit in their presentation box.

So, made-to-measure pastries were commissioned and biked round to the studio. They won the contract.

'It showed we had thought about his business and how we could help him,' says John Cousins.

Lesson: The more you know about new customers the easier it is to capture their interest and so win their business.

Customers Want a Partnership

In a highly competitive market, buyers want more than merely someone who supplies them with goods or services.

They are seeking a relationship with people they know, get along with and can trust. They want someone loyally fighting from *their* corner, on *their* side, and helping *them* do battle with rivals.

'The key thing people buy is a team they can work with,' says Charlie Makin, managing partner at media planners and buyers Kenny Lockett Booth. 'You need to send people to talk to the prospective client, to go through their research – to love them to death, really!'

Makin recalls how, while pitching for the British Home Stores account, one of their directors went to work behind the counter at BHS. 'The pitch went on for over a month and we were probably at the client's three times a week. Once you have a personal relationship going, that's half the battle.'

The importance of being seen as a member of their team is also stressed by Peter Bingle, of Westminster Strategy, who says that once his agency becomes a contender for a company's business: 'We'll almost regard them as a client and ensure anything we pick up that's of interest goes to them. It reinforces the message that we're already almost on board.'

ABOVE AND BEYOND NO. 1

On occasions fate can take a hand in helping persuade a prospective customer you are on their side. On the day his agency CKT, was pitching for the advertising business of an international retailer, managing director Paul Cowan spotted an armed raid in progress at one of their stores.

Despite being shot at, Paul chased after the robber and assisted in his arrest. A short time later a message was handed to the clients which read: 'We are so keen to win your business, one of our account directors managed to foil a raid on your local branch and get your money back. That's the kind of commitment we'll give you, we're a full service agency.'

Needless to say, they won the business!

Lesson: Seize every opportunity to impress a prospective client with your enthusiasm for winning their business.

ABOVE AND BEYOND NO. 2

When pitching for the job of publicising a major garden festival, PR company Rex Stewart were up against much larger consultancies. They knew that to stand any chance of success they must dare to be different. While other representatives arrived in business suits they turned up dressed as garden gnomes! It was not simply a memorable stunt but entirely appropriate to the business for which they were pitching. By showing themselves to be innovating, risk taking and relaxed, Rex and his team demonstrated the key benefits their prospective client sought. They won the business.

Lesson: Be willing to take a calculated risk to convince a new customer how well you understand their business.

Getting Inside Your Customer's Head

The only way to create a sales presentation that will persuade a new customer you are qualified to become a team player is to get inside their head.

To see the world through their eyes.

To hear it through their ears.

And the only way to achieve such an intimate understanding is *by doing your homework.*

The depth and breadth of your research will, of course, depend on how much profit you stand to make from a successful presentation. But, when assessing the likely profitability of any new business, take a long-term view, rather than focusing on immediate gains. As I explained at the start of this book, while face-to-face sales presentations rate as the most effective method for making sales, they are also the most costly. This means using them as a way not only of making that particular sale, but also as part of a strategy designed to win lifetime loyalty from the customer.

What You Need to Know

You should always start by obtaining basic information in the following three key areas.

1. The company

- How large is it?
- How profitable?
- Expanding or contracting?
- Privately owned or part of a group?
- Traditional or modern culture?

If, for instance, it is a manufacturing company do they handle all the processes from raw material to finished products or are the individual parts purchased outside the company and assembled on site?

Having established this basic framework, concentrate on. . .

2. Products and markets

- What product(s) or service(s) are provided?
- What is the company's standing in the market place?
- Is their market expanding or contracting?
- Is what they sell original and innovative or a derivative 'me-too' product or service?
- Is the currect financial climate hostile or supportive to their business?
- Who are their strongest competitors?

3. Who does the buying?

- Who takes purchasing decisions in your sales area?
- Who else might be involved in that decision?
- Who holds the real power within the company and what do you know about them?

Acting and Talking Like an Insider

The more you can discover about a potential client the easier it will be to talk to them in a language they can both understand and appreciate.

This is especially important when selling into a niche

market, such as government agencies. Such organisations usually have a particular outlook, culture and even language.

To become an insider, a team player regarded as deserving to be trusted with the new business, it is essential clearly to understand and empathise with their corporate culture. Talk and behave like an outsider and they are much less likely to place their trust in you. If, on the other hand, you quickly learn to 'talk their language', understand company jargon, in-jokes, and abbreviations employed for different products and departments, and are on friendly terms with the key personnel, you will rapidly be assimilated and accepted.

Advertising agency director Paul Cowan says: 'We follow a simple principle: once you've got a dialogue going with a potential client, be all over them like a cheap suit. You need to understand what lies behind the brief. We won't take on a pitch unless there's freedom of access. As much as anything else, we want to know we can work with the client. We wouldn't pitch if we didn't get on with the client, for example.'

WHAT IMPRESSES CUSTOMERS?

Research shows customers view these six qualities as keys to sales excellence:

- thoroughness and follow through;
- willingness to fight for the customer;
- full understanding of their needs;
- market knowledge plus a readiness to share it;
- substantial product knowledge;
- sound preparation of the sales presentation.

(**Source**: The Competitive Advantage, PO Box 10091, Portland, Oregon, 97210 USA)

Where to Find What You Need to Know

There are two main sources for researching new business:

- published records are available to anybody who knows where to look and what to look for;
- personal exclusive information obtained over the telephone or through face-to-face conversations.

Finding your way around published records requires knowledge and patience. Making the most of face-to-face or telephone conversations demands listening skills plus a knowledge of what questions to ask and when to ask them.

I shall describe practical techniques for positive listening in Chapter 5.

Published Sources

Business directories

These will tell you what achievements, if any, are credited to your potential customer. If the customer has written books or articles you should have at least a passing knowledge of them prior to the first meeting.

Business press

This includes such general interest business publications as *Fortune, International Business Week, Harvard Business Review, Sloane Management Review*, newspapers such as the *Financial Times* (UK) and *Wall Street Journal* (US), together with the business pages of serious newspapers.

It is worth while creating a cuttings library in your area of sales interest. Clip and file articles from relevant magazines and newspapers on a regular basis, not only about companies of immediate concern, but also in the general area of your business interests, for instance computing, electronics, finance, retailing and so on.

Keep yourself well informed about world trends likely to affect business by including news magazines such as *Time, Newsweek* and *The Economist* as part of your regular weekly reading.

To save precious time, skim read articles to identify those of possible interest, then clip and file for deeper study at a later date.

This is the method I use for extracting relevant information from the more than fifty newspapers and magazines I read each week.

Clipped material is placed in a folder which can be read, before being either discarded or refiled, when travelling by train or plane.

Business information on cassettes

A useful service for keeping busy executives up to date with all the latest trends and discoveries is offered by a New Jersey based company Newstrack Executive Tape Service.* They extract and record on cassettes articles and features from a wide variety of business sources. These can be played while driving or commuting, so turning what would otherwise be wasted time to profitable use.

Information on disc and CD-ROM

Many business and financial publications, including the London *Times* and *Sunday Times, Financial Times, The Economist, Time Magazine* and *Fortune*, plus an increasing number of other relevant magazines are available on computer disc or CD-ROM discs.

The latter require a special CD-Rom disc player which can either be fitted to your personal computer, in place of one

* Newstrack Executive Tape Service, 700 Black Horse Pike, Blackwood, NJ 08012, USA.

of the standard disc drives, or used as a stand-alone add-on. Although the investment required to set up such a service is fairly high, CD-ROMS provide a fast and convenient method of searching for a large amount of data.

Information on computer database

Many business-related magazines are available through on-line database, for example FT Profile (UK), Lexus/Nexus, Newsnet, Dow Jones News/Retrieval or Compuserve. These specialist news and information databases typically allow access to a wide range of sources, including wire services, Dow Jones, TASS and Associated Press, most major newsletter and company reports, as well as providing access to such services as Reuters Textline, Global Scan, Nikkei, ICC and Infocheck. Some publishers now make their publications available through databases, including McGraw-Hill which offers full-text, unedited articles from more than 45 technical publications covering fields as diverse as plastics and chemical engineering, coal and petrochemicals, securities and data communications.

Industrial research firms

Companies such as Mintel and credit checkers such as CCN (UK) and America's MDS Group provide a wide range of information about prospective customers, including their creditworthiness.

Fortune magazine offers a research service by fax–*Fortune* Company Profiles – covering thousands of US public companies, compiled from dozens of sources including Reuters and Standard and Poor's Disclosure. This can be faxed anywhere in the world.*

Trade press

The trade press provide detailed coverage in their specific sectors. Virtually every type of business in the world now has at least one magazine or newsletter devoted to their concerns.

* Call 0101 415 705 6973. Fax 0101 415 705 6969

Local newspapers

Even minor events and activities of companies in their circulation area are likely to be reported by local newspapers.

Unless you are doing major research on a company it is seldom worth investing the time and effort necessary to track down relevant stories in the local library or newspaper offices. If, however, you have time to spare before an appointment, studying the local press for news about the company being visited can prove productive.

In larger libraries the local paper, or papers, will be available on microfilm or fiche, so making your research faster and easier.

House journals

Published by most large organisations, house journals can often be obtained via a direct request to the public relations or press office of the company concerned. They provide a wealth of fascinating and invaluable information on products, achievements, promotions and company personnel. Apart from their factual content, such journals give you a feel for corporate culture. They can be entertaining, even slightly irrelevant, off-beat and creative, or plodding and worthy but devoid of wit. The chances are that their style reflects the culture of that company and the attitudes of senior management.

Dropping information gleaned from such sources into a preliminary conversation with your prospective customers can be a fast way of putting yourself on their side.

Personal Sources

Specialists

Cultivate people with insider knowledge of your industry. Talk to trade and business journalists, stockbrokers and analysts who cover that sector.

Joining the team

Although of limited application for most companies, sending salespeople to work for a prospective customer offers insights into their corporate culture and business methods which could not be obtained by any other method.

This research strategy is much used by public relations and advertising companies prior to a major pitch.

Biss Lancaster's chairperson Graham Lancaster recalls how, when his company was pitching for the Haagen Dazs ice-cream account: 'We spent a day behind the counter serving ice-cream. You pick up a culture and a language and a feeling of what the business is about.'

Telephone calls

This is an extremely powerful research tool which, when used correctly, allows you to bypass people such as secretaries, receptionists and personal assistants who – if dealt with face-to-face – might prove a significant obstacle to obtaining the knowledge you require.

I shall deal more fully with using the telephone in Chapter 6.

Junior employees

Cultivate receptionists, secretaries and telephone operators. Not only do they usually have an excellent grasp of what is going on within their company, but they are usually willing to chat about their organisation. Without suggesting or encouraging them to break confidences, a great deal of valuable knowledge can often be obtained.

Remember their first names, together with any personal details they may let slip. Learn to recognise their voices so that you can address them by name when phoning.

They can prove powerful allies in your quest to gain entry to the inside track and it is important to have them on your side.

'If you are pitching on their turf, you need their help and you don't want one of them badmouthing you because you've been rude to them,' says Paul Cowan. 'More importantly, you'll need access to their boss and they can either help or hinder.'

Management

Managers are another valuable source of the kind of insider knowledge which enables you to get inside your customer's head. Wining and dining an executive provides a convivial atmosphere in which to carry out such research, although there can be hidden hazards.

One sales director recalls the time his company was preparing a presentation for the marketing manager of a European travel company. 'He liked all our work – but he was single and lonely, and what he liked most was going to the wine bar. He always wanted his meetings at about 8.30 p.m., so he could go home, change and come back into town. Of course, this was the perfect way for us to learn all about his business, as he talked a lot when we wined and dined him. But in the end we had to put a stop to it because we discovered that he was a real nuisance with the girls!'

Buyers

Have as many interviews and briefings as you can get. It is the only way you will get to know who the different decision and policy makers within that company are.

One of the fastest ways of losing a sale is failing to identify exactly which person, or people, control the levers of power.

Talk to those who will be responsible for implementing any policies and recommendations you make or actually using the equipment you hope to supply. Discover any worries or inhibitions they may feel.

As I shall explain in Stage Three, all selling involves bringing about changes within an organisation and, unless you offer prompt and effective reassurance, such fears could cost you the deal.

One company selling word processors was on the point of

signing a major contract for the supply of personal computers when they suddenly found the deal going cold on them. Fortunately they had developed a friendly relationship with the office manager and, through her, discovered that the chairman's long-serving and much-respected secretary was technophobic. Her fear about not being able to master new technology lay at the root of their sales problems. The director loaned her a brand-new machine for home use over a long holiday weekend.

He had it delivered and installed by an extremely empathic and patient woman who not only demonstrated how easy it was to use, but reassured the woman by providing a role model. When the secretary returned after four days at the keyboard her fears had vanished and a contract was signed.

It is not uncommon to find middle managers who are able to exert a strong influence over whether or not your company gets the business, terrified of being cut out of the equation as you go straight to the chairperson.

Understand such concerns, by being well informed about internal office politics, and provide any reassurances that may be needed.

Failed sales presentations

Even the best presentations will not always win you new business. But while failure is never welcome, it can provide a valuable learning experience, teaching you how to avoid similar pitfalls and problems in the future.

Always ask the customer for feedback about why you failed to win their business. Usually you'll find them very forthcoming and helpful. Not only does this help you make your next presentation even more persuasive, but also leaves a positive impression with that client. By doing so you greatly increase your chances of winning new business from them on some future occasion.

Being sneaky

According to a top marketing manager, it's quite simple to get hold of either your client's or your competitor's literature. 'Posing as a student is the most standard way,' she says. 'All you need to do is ring the firm and say: "I'm a business student and I'm doing a paper on..." and they'll send you all their relevant information. It can be incredibly valuable to your pitch.'

Whether or not you feel such an underhand manoeuvre is either ethical or sensible must be left to your discretion.

But be aware this is not the only underhand tactic employed by both suppliers and buyers in their search for commercially valuable information.

The spy in the cab technique is an old favourite with certain advertising and PR people when they're desperate to find out how they fared in their presentation, and where the client is going next. The method only works on home territory, but if you don't feel guilty about adopting sneaky tactics, it can provide some very helpful feedback.

At the beginning of the meeting, confirm the 'housekeeping arrangements' with the client – in other words, what time will they be leaving your office. Ask if they'd like you to arrange a car to take them on to their next appointment or back to base. Then arrange for a member of your staff – or for a trusted driver – to take the wheel and eavesdrop.

A former employee of one major London advertising agency, who still uses the method as often as possible, describes how it works to his advantage: 'It gives you the inside track on the client's thinking, who's for you and who's against you,' he says. 'That allows you the opportunity to go back with other suggestions. If the client, for example, is overheard saying they hated the person presenting the creative work, we can then telephone and suggest that person may not be quite right for the account – without the client suspecting. We've certainly benefited from learning who else is on the pitch list. That helps because it gives you the chance to screw up the other agency's chances by giving the information to the trade press. That will put them in a rather uneasy position with the prospective client, who'll assume one of that agency's employees can't keep his or her mouth shut. We've also learned that some of the personalities on the team haven't worked as well as we thought. We've found out who our supporters are and then contacted them to encourage the relationship.'

If you think the spy in the cab and leaks to the trade press are unethical business practices, you should see some of the really dirty tricks some companies get up to.

A few years ago, two leading agencies were pitching against each other for a major animal charity.

A senior director at Agency A, who had good contacts within the media, tried to place a story stating that the chairperson of Agency B enjoyed shooting as a hobby. His intention was to send a cutting to the client suggesting, of course, that Agency B did not deserve their business.

Paul Cowan recalls being the victim of a dirty tricks campaign by a marketing manager who wanted to retain the existing advertising agency but had been ordered by the board of directors to review some others. Paul and his colleagues pitched for the business at 3 p.m., leaving behind their proposal document. This was handed to a freelance writer to plagiarise for good ideas on behalf of the other agency. Their rehashed version was then presented to the board the following morning.

Unfortunately, the ruse was rumbled when, by pure chance, Paul found himself travelling on the same train as an extremely tired freelance the following morning.

'He looked absolutely shattered and I asked him what he'd been doing and who for. When I heard that he'd been up all night working for this particular agency it all fell into place – but it was too late to do anything about it. I was delighted to hear that the marketing director had subsequently been fired.'

Giving Your Benefits Client Appeal

Because not all benefits have equal appeal, part of your research should be aimed at identifying those which have greatest attraction for your prospective customers.

It may be that such benefits are immediately obvious, but often their merits only become apparent after research and, when possible, consultation.

'The initial briefing is very important,' says Basil Towers, chairman and managing director of Christow Consultants. 'If you ask the right questions and probe deeply enough, the client will give you 90 per cent of the answers you need. The other 10 per cent is the ability to create an appropriate strategy and communicate it.'

During preliminary meetings ask open-ended questions starting with: How, What, When, Where, Who? The following suggested questions need not be asked in any particular order.

Ask: How much and how often do you buy?
Identifies: Sales potential and buying cycle.

Ask: How much do you know about my company/service?
Identifies: Extent of understanding of your products. This gives you the opportunity of describing benefits.

Ask: What company is supplying you at present?
Identifies: Current supplier, which may also tell you what level of service and quality you are competing against.

Ask: What other people will you have to consult about this decision or will have an input?
Identifies: Ways in which your benefits should be presented to meet that need. You can then ask a further 'What' question to seek information about their likely views on the matter.

Ask: When do you see this service/product as being needed?

Identifies: Time-scale and deadlines. At this point it may be apparent that your company cannot meet the terms demanded (see 'When to say no', below).

Ask: When would you like to take delivery?
Identifies: Point at which order will be current. This is a good closing question (see Stage Four).

Ask: Where do you see your company going? Where do you expect it to be in five years' time?
Identifies: Long-term potential.

Ask: Where else in your organisation might my product/service prove of value?
Identifies: Other opportunities within that company.

Ask: Who else is involved in the decision to buy?
Identifies: Key decision makers you will need to persuade.

Ask: Who outside your organisation do you think might be interested in my product/service?
Identifies: Further potential sources of new business.

Who is Doing the Buying?

Selling to single individuals with the power to buy offers both rewards and risks.

Only having to get inside the head of one person is an obvious plus point. And, provided that person is persuaded by your pitch, deals can often be done very rapidly.

On the other hand, should that person dislike you for any reason, the business is probably lost for ever no matter how effective your pitch.

Whether the decision to buy is taken by one person or a group – termed the decision-making unit (DMU) – depends on five factors:

The Price Tag

As the table below shows, the greater the cost the higher up an organisation you'll have to go to make your sales presentation.

Level of decision making

Expenditure	Board	Director	Manager
£50,000+	88%	11%	2%
Up to £50,000	70%	25%	4%
Up to £5,000	29%	55%	14%
Up to £2,500	18%	54%	24%
Up to £500	4%	31%	52%

(**Adapted from**: *How British Industry Buys*, survey by the Cranfield School of Management for the *Financial Times*, January 1984)

Only when the cost is less than £500 are more than 10 per cent of purchasing decisions taken at lower managerial or clerical level.

Originality

Since novelty involves a greater degree of risk, new and/or untested ideas must normally be approved at a higher level within a company than familiar and therefore commercially safer proposals.

Complexity

When technical issues are involved the agreement of specialists, either staff or independent consultants, may be required before your proposal can be accepted. There is an increasing trend in many companies to consult experts before buying a wide range of products, ranging from computers to catering services.

Although the agreement of these specialists is seldom final, a negative evaluation will clearly be unhelpful.

Because experts seek to justify their jobs, or fees, by weighing every opinion carefully, such consultations can significantly prolong the buying decision.

Corporate Culture

Many very large, overly bureaucratic, organisations appear to operate on what might be called a 'Yes ... but' principle. Each time somebody comes up with a new idea or fresh product there is a chorus of 'Yes ... but', followed by an avalanche of reasons for *not* making the proposed purchase. Perhaps the most common, if seldom openly voiced, reason is: 'Yes, but it wasn't invented here!'

Company Size

With a few exceptions where the company is led by a powerful, dictatorial individual a general rule is that the larger an organisation the more people will be involved in the decision-making unit.

Number of employees	Average number in DMU
Up to 200	3
201–400	5
401–1,000	6
1,000 plus	7

(Adapted from *Buying Influences by Company Size* (McGraw Hill))

Backing Up Your Claims

It's seldom enough just to *say* you can provide all the benefits your customer is seeking.

Most demand, if not proof, then considerable reassurance that you are capable of delivering on your promises.

This reassurance can consist of:

- endorsements from clients in similar fields;
- research data;
- examples of previous campaigns, projects, action plans, designs etc.

Of these, endorsements are the most important and persuasive, especially when selling to professionals, such as doctors, teachers, lawyers and so on, who generally rely on opinions of colleagues to a far greater extent than do businesspeople.

Perhaps they cynically suspect that endorsements by competitors, unless their personal friends, will be prejudiced by self-interest!

Despite this, third-party endorsements remain the best evidence that your service/product will meet their expectations.

Never be afraid to approach satisfied customers and ask either for a written endorsement or for permission to refer prospective clients to them for confirmation of your skills. A written endorsement is better for a number of reasons.

- It is easiest for them to provide and for you to use.
- It offers concise, clear-cut evidence in support of your claim. When speaking over the phone even a well-satisfied client may voice certain reservations or doubts – if only to protect themselves should something go wrong.
- It helps a rebuy. Committing yourself to anything makes it more likely you will see that to which you are expressing commitment in a favourable light. This is due to a process psychologists have termed *cognitive dissonance* and it works like this. Whenever our actions and thoughts are in conflict we experience discomfort or even considerable distress. To remove this disquiet we either change our actions or alter our attitudes.

Suppose you invest much time and energy in an activity, for example collecting bottle tops, that others regard as pointless. Will their criticisms make you view the pursuit as more or less important?

The answer is you are likely to become even more determined about the importance of that task since expending effort on an activity you accept as purposeless creates emotional conflict. This is why people under attack tend to become increasingly dogmatic and certain of themselves. This is an important point to bear in mind when dealing with objections to your proposals and one which I shall be dealing with in Stage Four.

By putting in writing what an excellent service you have provided your client comes to view your service as possibly even better than it actually was. This makes it more probable they will not only help you win new business, but also offer repeat business themselves.

When to Say No

If you do your homework properly there will be occasions, hopefully rare, when all the research points to one clear, if disagreeable, conclusion – you should not try and win this business. There are five occasions when this may happen.

- Your company lacks the necessary resources or expertise to do a first-class job.
- You have an existing customer who is a direct competitor.
- The remuneration is too low to make it profitable.
- You've got too much other work on to offer sufficient commitment.
- No genuine sales opportunity exists. Perhaps the company is satisfied with their present suppliers and is merely going through the motions of seeking a change. Or maybe the contract has been awarded, in all but fact, to friends of the chief executive.

Charlie Makin, managing partner at Kenny Lockett Booth Ltd, who plan and buy media space, says:

> 'There are some pitches where you know the odds are heavily stacked against you, such as when a marketing director really wants to work with another agency. You may only be on the list to make up numbers. But the one thing about new business is that there are no rules.
>
> 'Even if you've won four pitches in a row, it doesn't give you any more chance of winning the fifth. It all depends on the individual client.'

How It Looks from the Buyer's Side

So far in this chapter, I have concentrated on the sales presentation from your viewpoint.

But what do buyers want?

The following comments come from the marketing manager of an international food manufacturer and refer to his company's search for a new public relations consultancy.

However, much of what he says, particularly where pitfalls and mistakes to avoid are concerned, have general application. Key issues which apply to virtually every sales presentation are in (my) italics.

The Marketing Manager's Tale

> 'A team of us went to see a number of agencies at their premises. We prefer to do that as it gives you a better feel about the company.
>
> 'We then drew up a short-list of three, who came in to see us for a very specific brief on the way our business would be going next year.
>
> 'We also talked to them about how they would have improved on certain things we'd done.

'We gave them two to three weeks to respond and told them they would have an hour to make their presentations.

'*We were interested in strategic input, not flowery ideas.*

'Some agencies like to come in and talk to you during that time to get a feel for the business. Others are noticeable by their absence.

'One of these three was in here for at least two days, one asked a few questions over the telephone and the third was completely silent.

'Interestingly, the one that really messed up was the agency that was in here for two days.

'Our level of expectation of them may well have been higher because we believed we'd given them a tremendous insight into our business, more than any of the others, although they'd created that advantage.

'But they really *lacked any understanding*. There were some very fundamental things that I'd certainly told them which they either ignored or got completely wrong, and it affected the recommendations that they made. They actually finished third of the three.

'*It's all very well showing enthusiasm and asking the right questions, but if you don't log it and come back with the right answers it's a waste of time.*

'The agency that won the account was the one that asked a few interesting questions.

'*Their presentation was the most considered and thought-through and thought-provoking from our side. It was very professional.*

'The third agency was generally just lacking in comprehension and original ideas.

'They just replayed the current brief, plus a few ideas you can get from the top drawer.

'We'd asked them all to field the team they'd put on our business and that's important. We'd asked them not to go over the top with lots of glitzy slides, but they all presented on a video-screen system.

'We looked for a good understanding of our business, where we'd got to and where we are going, and the needs of our business.

'A good fit of people is important – and a good balance between the oily rags and the people who'll be at the top end of the business, the strategic, heavyweight people.

'Inevitably, we like to have an MD on board – we are a big client. It's very difficult for an agency to come in and hit all our criteria on the head at the same time.

'We have very high standards.

'What we expect is to have the impression of a good solid agency plus a degree of the unusual.

'We like to be excited by what we see and hear. If an agency just plays about with the brief and comes up with a workmanlike solid presentation you know they will do an effective job, but we expect to be excited by some original thinking.

'If an agency has done its homework, it has a certain confidence which comes through and, in a presentation, that confidence fuels a positive response from us, which in turn boosts their confidence – and the whole thing ends up on a high.

'If an agency isn't in tune with our business and during the presentation makes some comments or states some facts which aren't correct, they can perhaps tell that we're losing interest, looking at our watches and things like that.

'If there was to be a disaster with the slides, for example, we'd be relaxed about it. Everybody's been in that situation. If you blow an agency out because of that it's a bit unlucky.

'However, we had one guy who came in and presented on a unique form of merchandising. We thought it was a first-class presentation – well thought-through, punchy and thought-provoking, challenging and quite aggressive.

> 'We brought him back in to present to our sales and marketing director and he changed his whole presentation, which was against what we'd asked him to do.
>
> 'He'd toned it down, cut some of the corners – it was embarrassing and, needless to say, we haven't taken it any further.
>
> '*As a company we are keen on fostering long-term relationships. You get a much better result if you work with an agency for a long time. They understand what you want and they don't waste your time.*'

These comments can be summarised by what I term The Rule of Three. To make a successful sales presentation all must be obeyed:

1. know exactly what benefits you can offer;
2. understand your prospective customer's business;
3. appreciate your prospective customer's psychology.

By bringing these three elements together you will create a sales presentation that communicates the unique benefits you can offer in a way which is relevant, memorable and persuasive.

ACTION PLAN 5

If you have not already done so, start a cuttings library in your relevant sector of interest. Read as many general and specific business and trade publications as possible.

Aim to invest at least 5 per cent of your income on self-improvement, by subscribing to magazines, journals, buying books and taking courses.

ACTION PLAN 6

Take one company with whom you either currently do, or might one day do, business and practise carrying out research on them. Use as many of the sources listed in this chapter as possible. Build up a profile of that firm and its key personnel. Although intended as a training exercise, this often provides leads to new business opportunities.

KEY POINTS

- Only through careful research can you correctly identify those benefits which will be of greatest interest to a prospective customer.
- Once identified these benefits can be tailored to bring about the closest match between the customers' needs and what you can deliver.
- Your general knowledge should include a sound understanding of the business world, your company and its products, together with the latest sales techniques.
- Your specific knowledge should give you an insider's view of the prospective customer's corporate culture, aims and achievements.
- There are occasions when business should be declined. Your research should tell you when making a presentation will be a waste of time.
- Remember the Rule of Three, on which all successful sales presentations depend:
  - know what benefits you should offer;
  - know your prospective customer's business;
  - understand their buying psychology.

THE POWER OF POSITIVE LISTENING

'WE ARE BORN with two ears and one mouth. It pays to employ them in the same proportions.'

Anonymous

PRESIDENT Franklin D. Roosevelt had a theory that people never really listened to what he said and only praised his casual uttrances out of courtesy. To test his hunch he would sometimes greet guests: 'So good to see you. I murdered my grandmother this morning!'

Almost without exception the person would reply politely and approvingly. But he got caught out on one occasion when a woman nodded gravely before replying: 'Mr President, I'm sure she had it coming to her!'

The problem is this.

Hearing and listening are not one and the same thing.

Hearing is an ability the majority of us are fortunate enough to be born with.

Listening is a skill which must be learned, practised and perfected before it can be used successfully.

Listening is also a crucial part of the pre-presentation research process, since getting the brief right means asking the right questions – and listening for the right answers.

It's all too easy to turn a deaf ear to things that conflict with your preconceptions about the customer's needs and expectations.

The size of your customer's budget is an obvious source of misunderstanding and confusion. If you fail to listen carefully to financial constraints you could end up suggesting a champagne and caviar answer to a bread and butter problem.

Positive listening is also essential during the presentation itself and this means listening to your colleagues as carefully as the customer. For a common error in many otherwise well-prepared sales presentations is repetition or even contradiction of one another by different team members. By listening properly to associates you'll be able to pick up on things that went down well and avoid mines they may have stepped on.

So what does it take to listen in a powerful, positive and creative manner?

The first step is to break the habit of regarding talking as a worthier and more worthwhile skill than listening, and to realise that your ears can be more powerful than your mouth when it comes to winning new business.

As I stressed in the last chapter, successful selling means being able to see your message from the customer's viewpoint.

And this can only be achieved by listening so carefully that you not only hear what is being said, but also what is being implied and left unspoken.

As Peter Bingle, a director of Westminster Strategy, remarks: 'Too many people talk at, rather than to, people. It's important to let people finish asking and answering a question.'

Listening for Names

Listening becomes particularly important when it comes to remembering names. One of the main reasons people have difficulty recalling the name of someone they have just met is a failure not of memory but of listening.

When first introduced we are often so busy wondering what sort of person he or she is, whether or not we are attracted to them and if they like us in turn, that their name never properly registers.

WHAT'S IN A NAME?

A PR company was asked to 'rescue' a client from a long-running vendetta by a journalist since the bad publicity was affecting their trade. They decided to set the record straight by offering an 'exclusive' interview with the managing director. When the journalist arrived the PR was struck by his rodent-like features.

Unfortunately he allowed this thought to slip through his lips and introduced the journalist to this client as Mr Weasel.

Everyone laughed – except for the journalist who took his revenge by writing a scathing article. Soon after, the PR company lost the account.

Lesson: Speaking without thinking is like shooting without aiming.

Most people are extremely sensitive about their names and feel offended if these are forgotten, mispronounced or misspelled. The only way of avoiding this social hazard is by listening attentively when told a name, silently repeating it several times, confirming the pronunciation whenever the name is hard to say and using it several times in the conversation which follows.

Status Affects Listening Ability

As the table below, based on research conducted by the Savage-Lewis Corporation of Minneapolis, shows, the effectiveness of communications diminishes with every step down the corporate hierarchy.

	Speaking to		Level of understanding
Director	_______	Director	90%
Board chairperson	_______	Vice-president	67%
Vice-president	_______	General manager	56%
Foreperson	_______	Worker	20%

This is a difficulty which has to be borne in mind when dealing with a buyer whose status you perceive to be far greater than your own.

Train yourself to ignore the trappings and aura of power with which, for example, a celebrity CEO may surround him, or herself, and concentrate hard on what is being said.

How Relevant is the Message – The WIIFM Factor

The only person most people are really interested in is *themselves*! When American researchers analysed 500 phone calls they found the word 'I' had been used more than 4,000 times!

Human nature dictates, therefore, that we are going to pay the closest attention to things which appear most relevant, interesting and rewarding, and least to messages which seem to have little or no personal significance.

This is sometimes called the WIIFM – or 'What's in it for me? – factor.

WE HEAR WHAT WE WANT TO HEAR

A naturalist and a businessman were walking together along a busy city street. Passing a derelict, overground building site the naturalist suddenly paused. 'Listen', he said in delight, 'a cricket singing.'

'I can't hear anything,' the businessman objected. Then nodding towards the hurrying crowd he added: 'And neither can anybody else.'

The naturalist took a coin from his pocket and let it drop to the pavement. At the slight clink of metal on stone a dozen heads immediately turned.

'What you hear,' said the naturalist, 'depends on what you want to hear.'

As an example, consider that most uninterested of all audiences, airline passengers, being given the routine pre-take off safety lecture by cabin crew. While being given information about the location of exits, how to use oxygen masks or fit life-jackets, the vast majority do anything and everything except listen. They read, chatter, stare out of the window and even listen to personal stereos. Frequent travellers, I suspect, do it to demonstrate their blasé approach to flying, while first-timers want to appear like frequent fliers!

Now consider how they might respond to the same

information were an emergency to arise. With the aircraft plunging earthwards knowing where the exits are and how to adopt the bracing position would become a major priority, and would be listened to with intense interest.

The care with which we listen is also related to the personal significance we attach to a particular communication. The greater its relevance the more closely we attend.

A key purpose of your preliminary research is to pinpoint the benefits you have on offer which will have the greatest WIIFM appeal. While doing your homework keep in mind the WIIFM factor. Put yourself in your prospective customer's shoes by asking yourself: 'What's in it for them?'

Why Speech Speed Drives Us to Distraction

One problem with concentrating on the spoken word is that our brain is capable of processing speech far more rapidly than people can talk. During normal conversation people often speak at less than 100 words per minute. Even a TV racing commentator going flat out seldom exceeds 200 words per minute, yet we can understand sentences spoken at more than twice that speed.

To add to the risk of becoming distracted, normal conversations are full of repetition; the same idea may be restated several times or repeated in a number of slightly different ways. Then there are sounds and phrases such as 'umm ... er ... mmmm' and phrases like 'you see ...', 'I mean ...' and 'you know ...'

When listening to a radio or television interview, notice how frequently interviewees start their response with: 'Well ...', often followed by a slight pause.

All these phrases provide an extra second or so of time in which the speaker can gather his or her thoughts.

Slow speech, repetition, redundancy and meaningless

sounds can quickly drive all but the most skilled and dedicated listener to distraction. Yet by allowing yourself to be distracted you run the risk of false assumptions and significant misunderstanding. Avoid this trap by listening actively. While continuing to play close attention, ask yourself such questions as:

> 'How does his remark influence the way I should describe the benefits on offer?'
>
> 'In what ways could this opinion affect her decision to buy?'
>
> 'Who else in the company is likely to hold the same views?'

These silent queries help check your understanding of what's been said as well as making the key points raised easier to remember. Notice, too, any hesitations, pauses, meaningful silences, changes in emphasis and speed of delivery. They often betray the emotions bubbling away beneath the surface of the conversations. These are emotions which often tell you far more about a person's true feelings on a subject than the words actually spoken.

We will now look at some of the negative ways in which people listen.

The Hazards of Negative Listening

The three most frequently encountered types of unhelpful listening are as follows.

Distracted Listening

This occurs whenever we attempt to attend to two tasks simultaneously.

A classic exponent of this is the marketing director of a major UK financial institution who, by his own admission, is a good talker and a bad listener. He once warned a meeting of marketing agencies that if he stopped talking it wasn't because he was listening to what was being said, but because he was thinking about what to say next!

More commonly, the distracted listener is trying to do some other mentally challenging task, such as preparing a report, checking correspondence or working on accounts at the same time.

Instead of stopping and paying attention, you listen with half an ear to what's being said and often offer an opinion or agree a course of action on the basis of that partially attended to exchange.

Distracted listening is especially common when using the phone, since the other person cannot watch you reading papers, signing letters, checking your mail, tidying your desk, and performing a hundred and one usually unnecessary and always distracting tasks.

Avoid this trap by setting clear priorities.

If your current activity takes precedence over a conversation, it is far more efficient and courteous to explain, politely but firmly, that you are unable to give their comments the attention they deserve. Then arrange a time when you are able to give the other person your undivided attention.

Far from being annoyed, the other person is usually flattered that you are treating their ideas or problems seriously. When the other person has something to say which has a higher priority or urgency than your current activity, stop what you are doing completely and give them your undivided attention.

Red buttons and green flags

Attempting to do two things at once is not the only cause of distracted listening. Strong emotions create an equally powerful barrier to comprehension. We are quite incapable of listening positively when anxious or angry.

This is an important cause of the mistakes found in

communications between two people of markedly different status. Apprehension about being in the presence of somebody viewed as being so much more important and powerful than oneself not only ties the tongue but blocks the ears.

We all have little red buttons, in other words, ideas, opinions or attitudes which trigger such a powerful emotional response we become too aroused to listen positively.

Such emotions cause us to attend primarily to any information which appears to confirm assumptions made about the other person.

Manipulative people may deliberately press one of our red buttons in order to gain a psychological advantage.

Whenever you feel your emotions taking command, breathe deeply, then count slowly to five while exhaling. At the same instant tell yourself firmly but silently 'Stop!'

Since it is impossible to hold more than one thought at a time in conscious awareness the angry reaction will, at least temporarily, be brought to a halt. This technique can also be used during diagnostic listening (see below).

If you still feel too emotional to listen objectively, make an excuse to take a break. Even a brief respite makes all the difference to the level of concentration you can bring to an exchange.

You will find strategies for controlling anxiety and stress in Stage Four.

Green flags are another emotional trap. These comprise lavish praise and compliments on our performance. While obviously making for more agreeable listening than red buttons, green flags are just as disruptive to concentration. Fulsome flattery has a tendency to deafen one to any sting in the tail of the speaker's remarks. This can lead you to miss vital parts of the communication.

The more your heart swells with pride and pleasure, the less attention is paid to any less palatable aspects of their message.

'You've done a terrific job for us over the past year. The board are delighted and asked me to let you know how highly your services have been appreciated and valued. But I'm afraid cutbacks mean we'll have to ask for a one third reduction in your fees if you want to retain our business next year!'

Hearing such lavish praise, the WIIFM factor causes you to focus on the compliments and pay little or no attention to the sting in the tail. It may only be after you have committed your company to an unprofitable contract that the full impact of what has been said sinks in.

Protect yourself against the hidden menace of the green flag by first acknowledging the complimentary remarks and then moving to a neutral topic while regaining your composure. Direct the exchange back to serious matters only when fully in control of your emotions.

Dismissive Listening

This happens whenever you've already made up your mind what the other person is attempting to say. A frequent complaint of customers and clients is that salespeople do not pay sufficient attention to their true needs. All too often they seem to adopt the attitude: 'Here is the answer, now what is your problem?'

During dismissive listening you attend only to information which confirms or supports your immediate idea. A frequent result is a sales presentation which bears little or no resemblance to the client's real needs. The benefits offered are either so general or wide of the mark they fail to satisfy the customer's WIIFM factor.

'Salespeople are so busy trying to sell us some off-the-shelf answer, they don't seem to listen to what we need,' complained the director of a major fancy goods manufacturer.

'When we wanted to put in a new computer system, for example, six potential suppliers were approached. Their representatives came to see us, and listened with apparent interest and attention to our explanations of the type of system required.

'They went away and, except in one case, produced proposals which failed to meet even our basic criteria on speed, price, delivery targets and so forth. Presumably they had heard what we said, but they certainly hadn't been listening.'

This is an easy trap to fall into if you are convinced *your* product or service is superior to anything else on the market – an attitude I term the 'better mousetrap' fallacy. No matter how superior they may seem to you, benefits which lack relevance to your customer's needs are not benefits at all. Indeed, a product or service which offers fewer, less impressive, benefits may match their needs far more closely. Avoid dismissive listening by approaching every meeting with an open mind.

While it is never possible to be entirely neutral, try not to arrive for your first meeting preprogrammed with a set of assumptions about your customer's needs. Keep yourself alert by using diagnostic and reflective listening (see below) to establish exactly which benefits are likely to prove most attractive to that particular company or individual.

Judgemental Listening

This involves passing judgement before much, if anything, has been said. It appears to be a fundamental fact of human nature that we do make up our minds about others very rapidly (see Stage Four).

This arises through a tendency to pigeon-hole people on the basis of very few clues, the majority non-verbal. Height, body shape, hair and skin colour are among the physical attributes we use to reach conclusions about personality and intelligence.

Tall people are seen as confident and assertive, plump individuals as affable but unambitious, redheads are believed to have fiery tempers, spectacle wearers are seen to be intelligent and so on.

Similarly, if somebody speaks with what we infer to be an

uneducated voice, they tend to appear less bright, while if their voice is low and their delivery slow they may be viewed as tough and confident, but not especially quick-witted.

These assumptions exert a powerful influence over the way the content of people's conversations are judged. When speaking to somebody whose intelligence and erudition (however mistakenly) we admire, their most trivial utterance, no matter how crass, is treated with a degree of respect not afford to those whose IQ and knowledge we assume to be meagre.

Avoid this trap by using the technique of empathic listening described below.

Although I have described these three types of listening separately, they are seldom so cleanly and neatly categorised in real-life encounters.

Distracted listening can cause you to make judgements about the other person, which may then result in dismissive listening. Similarly, negative assumptions about the merit or significance of what you are being told will quickly result in distracted listening.

The only way to prevent these barriers to understanding is by using positive listening.

The Power of Positive Listening

Positive listening involves listening not only to what's said but also paying attention to those words left unspoken. This means use your eyes as well as your ears. The three main ways to listen positively are by diagnostic, reflective and empathic listening.

Diagnostic Listening

Here you listen to a client in the same way a good physician listens to patients when probing for symptoms.

You remain non-judgemental because any comments, especially criticisms, will inhibit the other person's flow of ideas and increase their reluctance to address the deeper issues, so making it harder to get to the root of their needs.

Pay attention to the other person's tone of voice. Conflict between what is said and how those words are spoken provides clues to painful emotions simmering below the surface.

Be alert for jokes, especially self-deprecating ones. When enquiring about the possibility of supplying artwork for an upcoming conference, a freelance designer told his friend at the production company: 'I wouldn't stand a chance...'

This was misinterpreted as betraying a lack of interest in the work rather than a tactic for reducing the stress of voicing a request which might be refused.

Humour is often used to protect oneself against the fear of rejection, expressing an embarrassing idea or describing anxiety-arousing feelings.

Pay close attention to expression, gestures and posture. Physical tension or anxious fidgets betray emotional stresses. Notice, too, any pauses, hesitations or repetitions that are often caused by anxiety.

In the back of your mind use the same phrase employed to explain benefits to a client, 'which means that...'. Each time the other person mentions a key issue or problem, say to yourself 'which means that...', which will help pinpoint the underlying source of their problem and the reason why they may be interested in what you have to offer.

These three words can be the key which unlocks the door on the benefits they really seek, but may not even be fully aware of requiring.

Take, for instance, the case where a would-be purchaser of catering services tells you: 'At present each of our six factories is responsible for running their own staff canteens...'

'Which means that...'

Probably this means a duplication of effort, spiralling costs, little or no central control, variable food quality and so forth.

While your potential client may be aware of some of these problems, it's quite likely that they do not know about them all.

Reflective Listening

This means paraphrasing and repeating back what has been said. This has a number of important consequences.

The first is to confirm your understanding of what has just been said. This prevents wasteful mistakes being made at the very start of your relationship; errors which could quite easily cost you a lucrative pitch.

If a misunderstanding has arisen, reflective listening traps it at a very low level in the communication before any harm can be done.

Sometimes it also prevents an error being made by the client who, until that moment, had not realised his or her blunder.

The mistake may be one of factual accuracy: 'Good heavens, did I say 20,000 tonnes? That should have been 200,000 tonnes!'

More often, however, it is one of interpretation. Until the idea was repeated back to the speaker, he or she was not fully aware of the true implications.

A second valuable benefit of listening reflectively is that any strong emotions attached to an idea tend to be reduced once the concept has been placed in the public arena through paraphrase and repetition.

This makes it easier for the speaker to put their proposals into perspective. While every phrase and sentence should not be reflected back, it is helpful to summarise key concepts and paraphrase any complex thoughts to check your understanding. Reflective listening is a powerful tool for combating any lingering objections which are preventing you from closing a deal, a problem I shall discuss further in Stage Four.

Empathic Listening

This means putting yourself in the other person's position, so far as one is ever able, to see the situation through their eyes and hear it through their ears. Viewing events from their side of the desk makes it easier to appreciate the pressures and constraints – financial, personal, cultural – the other person is operating under and easier to tailor your benefits to meet those needs.

Empathic listening also allows you to identify that individual's favoured style of communication, based on whether their personality profiles match that of a triangle, square, squiggle or circle (as used in the test at the start of this book). Identifying the personality type of your prospective customer can, however, provide crucial pointers about how best to tailor your presentation (see Stage Four).

By developing the powerful skill of positive listening you can become an even more efficient communicator.

Finally, always keep in mind these six basic rules for positive listening.

1. Before starting any type of conversation be clear in your own mind what it is you hope to achieve. Ask yourself 'What do I expect to gain by listening?'
2. Take the lead in conversations whenever possible as this gives you a psychological advantage. Whoever starts a communication is in a stronger position to direct it along the lines most favourable to them. You will also find it easier to end the exchange, once the purpose has been achieved, so gaining the advantage of having the last word.
3. If the other person is shy, reticent or not especially

articulate, smooth their flow both verbally, by using brief comments such as 'I see...' or 'I understand...' and non-verbally, with smiles, nods, eye-contact and looking interested. When encouraged to chatter people often say, and betray, far more than they intended.

4. Never be afraid to check your understanding of these six basic questions – Who? What? When? Where? Why? How? They'll ensure you've fully and accurately understood the message.
5. Pay attention to pauses, hesitations or repetitions, all of which are often caused by anxiety. They could indicate that the person is being less than honest with you.
6. Always talk less than you listen when laying the groundwork for a pitch. Most people so dislike silences they'll rush to fill them with words, any words, often indiscreet words!

   The deliberate silence is a technique much used by expert interviewers – journalists and police officers – to encourage self-disclosure. Sales professionals will also confirm that you can talk a prospect out of closing on a deal by saying even one word more than is necessary.

ACTION PLAN 7

Test your listening ability with this questionnaire. Use the results to help you identify current strengths and weaknesses in this vital sales skill.

Tick the appropriate statement:

1. I follow my hunches:

(a) *frequently* ☐ (b) *occasionally* ☐ (c) *seldom or never* ☐

2. I play a sport or perform some other activity better in public:

(a) *frequently* ☐ (b) *occasionally* ☐ (c) *seldom or never* ☐

3. I prefer working in a neat and tidy office:

(a) *seldom or never* ☐ (b) *occasionally* ☐ (c) *always* ☐

4. I prefer listening to talking:
(a) *frequently* ☐ (b) *occasionally* ☐ (c) *seldom or never* ☐

5. When arguing I find myself wandering from the point:
(a) frequently ☐ (b) *occasionally* ☐ (c) *seldom or never* ☐

6. I prefer to work in a group rather than on my own:
(a) *frequently* ☐ (b) *occasionally* ☐ (c) *seldom or never* ☐

7. I enjoy doing things on the spur of the moment:
(a) *frequently* ☐ (b) *occasionally* ☐ (c) *seldom or never* ☐

8. If taking directions I prefer to sketch a plan rather than write notes:
(a) *frequently* ☐ (b) *occasionally* ☐ (c) *seldom or never* ☐

9. When somebody is sad I feel unhappy too:
(a) *frequently* ☐ (b) *occasionally* ☐ (c) *seldom or never* ☐

10. Bad news on TV makes me feel depressed:
(a) *frequently* ☐ (b) *occasionally* ☐ (c) *seldom or never* ☐

Score: Award 2 points for each (a); 1 for (b)s and 0 for (c)s.

20–15: You are empathic and sensitive. While this helps you share others' feelings, it also prevents your being sufficiently objective on occasions. Practise developing your analytical powers to avoid being overly influenced by the emotional content of communications. Pay particular attention to perfecting diagnostic listening skills.

8–14: You have the potential to be both an empathic and objective listener. Use the procedures described in this chapter to enhance these skills still further.

0–7: You are a logical listener, who excels when dealing with factual conversations, but could miss the equally significant emotional undercurrents. Work on developing your empathic listening skills more fully.

KEY POINTS

- Listening is not the same as hearing. Positive listening is a skill that must be learned and practised.
- Avoid the negative listening traps of being distracted, dismissive or judgemental. Approach each conversation with an open mind.
- Be aware of your red buttons – things said which create powerful emotions. And beware of green flags. Praise can sometimes deafen you to criticisms.
- Positive listening can be diagnostic, reflective or empathic.
- Listen beneath the surface of the words. Often the most important part of a spoken message is conveyed by pauses, changes in emphasis, hesitations and other non-verbal utterances. And watch body language too, especially changes in posture indicating tension or lack of interest (see Stage Four for more on this).

PLUGGING IN TO PHONE POWER

'WE HATE to run, but Herbert likes to get home in time to slam the phone down on a few telemarketing calls.'

Cartoon caption, New Yorker Magazine Inc., 1988

DESPITE what the *New Yorker* said about telemarketing, your telephone can prove one of the most powerful weapons in your sales armoury. It is a device with the potential to open almost any door. And when it comes to winning new business, getting in is everything.

Consider the advantages it has over any other form of communication:

- the telephone allows direct contact with prospective clients;

- you can communicate faster and more efficiently by phone or fax than in any other way;
- the phone often enables you to contact executives who might refuse a face-to-face meeting;
- the telephone is your company's front-line ambassador for the majority of those doing, or seeking to do, business with you.

Used correctly the telephone can reduce stress, increase efficiency, and can add more hours and greater profit to your working week.

But beware.

The telephone is a two-edged weapon capable of losing you business and goodwill every bit as swiftly and surely as it will help you win them. I have calculated that as much as 25 per cent of turnover can be lost through poor telephone technique.

If that sounds improbable consider this.

A recent survey by the research company Teleconomy found that of 3,000 calls made to 300 different companies, the vast majority failed to elicit a civilised response.

Over a third of calls rang more than eight times before being picked up and three-quarters of those connected were greeted with an off-hand salutation. Only 1 per cent received an apology for being kept waiting.

For the lucky ones who actually made it through the first hurdle of the switchboard and got put through to the right extension, more barriers to business were erected.

Callers were left holding while the right person was tracked down; very few were given an instant answer to their query and 44 per cent of callers who asked to be called back by someone who could provide answers to their query were totally ignored.

If you think that could never happen in your company try this experiment. Call in from an outside line with a tricky request.

Give a name that's hard to pronounce and remember,

then ask to speak to someone who can help you solve your problem. You will probably be surprised, and shocked, at how easy it is to lose a potential customer.

Winning with Phonepower

In the century or so since a teacher of the deaf named Alexander Graham Bell invented the phone while trying to construct a hearing aid, the telephone has become so familiar we take it for granted.

And because it is so easy to use many make the mistake of assuming it is equally easy to use well.

Good telephone technique, however, requires time and practice to perfect. Once mastered it will prove a potent ally in your fight to win new business and retain the loyalty of existing customers.

Personality and Phonepower

The way you use the phone and your attitude towards it depends on certain of your personality traits as explored in the shape test at the start of this book which works by tapping unconscious motivations. Although quick and easy it has proved remarkably helpful in tailoring communications which best match an individual's approach to life.

What Your Choice Reveals

△ If you chose the triangle you can best be described as a *go-getter*. The only symbol with a clear sense of direction, this is the first choice of high achievers. You set yourself clear goals in life and work single-mindedly towards them.

○ If you chose the circle you are more likely to be a *mediator*. The circle's perfect harmony attracts those with a warm and warm and empathic personality whose skill lies in dealing with people. An intuitive understanding of others makes you a skilled and persuasive negotiator.

~ The squiggle is the first choice of a *dynamo*. This eccentric symbol is favoured by those who thrive on variety and like being involved in a great many activities at the same time. Enthusiastic and bursting with energy, you are attracted by novel tasks and unfamiliar challenges.

□ Finally, the square is most often chosen by a *scientist*. The logic of this symbol appeals to objective thinkers who analyse problems carefully and reach their conclusions methodically. You base judgements on facts and figures, rather than hunches or guesswork. The telephone smooths your working day by offering immediate access to a number of information sources.

Although most people are a mixture of all four symbols, research suggests that people generally prefer one or two far more than the others.

Your first choice reveals the most dominant aspect of your personality.

The second symbol indicates a less powerful but still influential aspect of your character. For example, you could be a go-getter at work but a mediator at home.

Recognising Personality Types

You can hardly ask prospective customers to take this test – although some of the sales professionals to whom I have taught the simple test actually use it as an amusing and often insightful way of breaking the ice. After all, as I explained in the previous chapter, nothing fascinates us so much as learning something new about ourselves!

Fortunately it is not always necessary to use the drawn symbols to identify which one a person would make his, or her, first choice. The way in which language is used can often provide the same insights.

Go-getters (triangles) use the language of achievement. They speak of 'setting goals', 'working towards objectives', 'planning ahead', 'making progress' and 'moving forward'. Their tone is brisk, business-like and purposeful. They'll finish your sentence impatiently and end the call abruptly once they've achieved their purpose.

Mediators (circles) use phrases such as 'My feeling is. . .', 'My intuition is. . .', 'I sense that. . .', 'My gut reaction is. . .', and 'I've a hunch that. . .'. They talk slowly and quietly, listening carefully to what you have to say and paying close attention to your views.

Dynamos (squiggles) use phrases which convey enthusiasm and energy. They'll tell you 'It sounds great', 'This is a really exciting project', 'I'm thrilled by the idea', 'You are going to love this'. They talk quickly, urgently, excitedly, with ideas often tumbling over one another, such is their speed of delivery.

Scientists (squares) favour remarks like 'Let's consider the facts', 'Speaking objectively', 'Logic demands', 'The way I figure it' and 'I think we must', They speak slowly and carefully, reflecting on their words, and instantly correcting any mistakes you may make.

How to Talk to Them

Now we've got a better idea of how to recognise them, here are a few tips on how to talk to the different personality types, either over the phone or face-to-face.

Go-getters Be brisk, direct and to the point. Time wasters are most unpopular. Have a clear idea of what you want from the call before dialling. Stress how your ideas can help them attain goals or make more efficient use of their time. Your tone must sound brisk and confident.

Mediators They want even business calls to be sociable. Take time to chat in a friendly fashion.

Ask about their health, how their children are doing in

school, discuss the weather. Take time to listen to their ideas or problems. Your tone should be warm and empathic.

Dynamos Enjoy plenty of variety in their conversations. Don't be afraid to introduce several different topics or to jump from one idea to the next. Remember, they are quickly bored. Speak in a lively, enthusiastic manner which conveys a sense of urgency and excitement.

Scientists Expect you to keep social chat to a minimum and provide relevant facts and figures precisely. If you don't know an answer say so honestly rather than taking a guess. Say you'll find out and phone back. Speak firmly, clearly and unemotionally. Confirm key points with a faxed summary.

Taking Control – Keeping Control

The secret of success when researching or selling over the telephone is always to feel in control of the call.

This means controlling both your own emotions and the content, direction and final destination of the exchange.

I shall start by considering emotions since these are often the hardest to master.

Anxiety-Arousing Calls

How tense or confident you feel will depend on three variables:

- the type of call being made;
- whom you are phoning;
- previous experience in making that type of call.

Fear of rejection means that, for newcomers to selling, cold calling – where a possible consumer is telephoned out of the blue – is the toughest, most nerve-racking type of call to make (see below).

Anxiety over being rebuffed prevents the cold caller coming across as confident and authoritative, so increasing the likelihood of the very rejection they feared in the first place. As anxiety levels rise, concentration slips and the ability to communicate the benefits that can be offered sharply declines.

For people whose business is not professional selling, calls which demand any form of cold pitching can be daunting and disagreeable. And some small businesses, which cannot afford to employ full-time, trained telesales staff, lose a huge amount of sales as a result of this diffidence.

The secret of telephone success is to stay in control of your emotions. If tension is allowed to build, concentration slips and your ability to communicate nose dives. Bodily tension also makes your voice different.

Research shows that a tense man sounds elderly, irritable and inflexible, while tense women are judged to be emotional, irrational and dim.

Banish tension by relaxing mind and muscles prior to making a challenging call. Here's how to unwind quickly and discreetly while still seated at your desk.

Calm down before calling

To bring anxiety under control before attempting a challenging call use this rapid relaxation technique.

- Deliberately tighten your muscles. Clench your fists, curl your toes, stretch your legs, flatten your stomach and take a deep breath. Hold this tension for a slow count to five.
- As you slowly exhale, allow your body to go limp. Drop your shoulders, unclench your fingers and flop out in the chair.
- Now take another deep breath and hold this for five seconds. While exhaling keep your jaw loose and teeth unclenched.
- Breathe quietly for five seconds and feel a sense of deep calm flow through your whole body.

- Finally, unwind mentally by picturing yourself lying on the golden sand of a sun-warmed beach by a clear, blue ocean. Hold this image for a few moments, then, without further hesitation, dial the number and make the call.

If you are on the telephone for lengthy periods, use shoulder and neck rolls between calls should any part of your body become tense.

The Menace of Microphone Fright

One common but infrequently recognised reason why inexperienced phone users become overly anxious is a phenomenon broadcasters call microphone fright. As producers know to their cost, bright, articulate and successful people can turn into incoherent wrecks when asked to do a live radio interview.

For some people, using the phone can have the same effect if not usually to the same extent.

Telephone fright reveals itself by a loss of fluency, quick-wittedness and confidence rather than incoherence.

If this is a problem for you, try these tips for developing professional expertise.

Picture your caller

Never talk 'at' the handset. Instead, imagine the person you are calling is sitting opposite. Now speak to him, or her, directly. Picture their likely responses to your remarks. See them smiling at your witticisms or beaming with pleasure as you pay a compliment.

If you know what the other person looks like, picturing them vividly ought not to be hard.

Some salespeople find it helpful to place a photograph of their favourite person, boy or girlfriend, husband, wife, Mum or Dad, on the desk in front of them and address their remarks to the photograph.

When talking to a stranger try creating a mental image of

what they might look like, based on their voice. If deep and sonorous, they may have a big build. When light and hesitant, the speaker is more likely to be a slightly built, somewhat diffident individual.

Use body language

While talking over the phone use the same body language as you would during a face-to-face meeting. If your usual conversational style involves lots of gestures and facial expression that's how you should talk when phoning. Not only does this improve the pace and flow of speech, but by mirroring emotions in your face and body you will make your voice sound far more relaxed, confident and natural.

Smile as you dial

Smiling while phoning not only makes you sound warmer, more enthusiastic and friendly, but also helps boosts energy levels. A smile releases brain chemicals which make us feel more confident and optimistic.

Cultivate a good voice

Talk slowly, since people obviously cannot understand something they are unable to hear easily. By talking slowly you will also sound friendlier and less threatening. Rapid delivery conjures up an image of the 'fast-talking, not-to-be-trusted salesperson' in many minds.

Speak loudly enough to be heard, since asking you to repeat something irritates prospects and wastes everybody's time. Unfortunately, anxious people tend to talk rapidly and softly, a combination that is the kiss of death to sounding persuasive and confident. Sounding friendly will also warm your voice up, making you sound more trustworthy and reliable – two of the quaities we naturally associate with our friends.

If you are uncertain about your voice quality, practise with a tape recorder and listen critically to the results. Get friends and relatives to listen too, and score yourself marks out of ten on these five key points:

- friendliness
- confidence
- clarity
- speed of delivery
- diction and pronunciation.

Ask 'Will that be all right?'

A one-year study conducted by the Equitable Life Assurance Society has clearly demonstrated that using the simple phrase – 'Will that be all right?' – can significantly enhance your success by:

- inviting the prospect to respond to you and start a dialogue, but in a friendly, non-threatening manner;
- bringing the prospect back into the conversation at any point where *you* need feedback or to reinforce a key part of the message;
- subtly compelling the prospect to agree with your proposition by responding 'Yes, that will be all right.' This reponse is the most likely one, since people almost always do what is easiest. It takes a very stubborn person to respond negatively to such a cordial enquiry. And the more times they answer yes, the greater your chances of success;
- it can be used as a close to gain agreement from the prospect at a later stage in the interview. If you have employed it a couple of times already, the prospect's mind-set will be such that a slightly trickier or more demanding request is also likely to trigger the positive response.

In some cases the prospects have been found to like this phrase so much that they even copy the cadence and voice tone of the person using it. 'Will that be all right?' is an excellent example of a technique which helps ensure that you stay in command of the situation. For it is only by being in control of the conversation that you can take it in the required direction.

Controlling Content

Here are a dozen more practical ways to control the conversation and direct it along the lines most favourable to your sales purpose.

1. Seize the Initiative

Do this by initiating sales and research calls whenever you can. This places you at a psychological advantage for three reasons.

- *You* have decided to take up the other person's time and they have agreed to let you do so. By accepting your call, therefore, the other person has allowed him or herself to be, at least temporarily, dominated.
- Because you can choose how the conversation starts you have a better chance of directing it along the most advantageous lines.
- Finally, whoever initiates a call is in the strongest position to end it without causing offence, so saving you valuable time.

Have a clear objective of what you want to achieve from the call before ever dialling the number.

Keep a note of any information you have about the company being called, together with brief details of organisations you helped in similar situations or lines of work.

Always begin by saying good morning or good afternoon for the reasons given above. The phrase gives the person answering time to tune in to your name, which should be given in full, and the full name of the person you are calling.

Never ask 'Is so and so in today?' or 'Please may I speak to so and so?' If you do the receptionist is likely to screen out your call. And, unless you are personal friends with the person being called, never ask for them by their first name.

Only give your company's name if it is very well known. Instead, say something vague, but never evasive, such as:

'I represent a consultancy specialising in taxation matters.'

Never ask 'How are you?' since it simply sounds phoney and too much like a cheap sales pitch.

Never say 'You don't know me' (see 'Cold calling'), as it merely sounds weak, wimpish and utterly lacking in confidence.

2. Check Your Timing

Plan the timing of your calls carefully. Executives are often more approachable out of normal office hours when their secretaries are away from their desk, i.e. before 9 a.m., after 5 p.m. and during the lunch break.

The worst time to call is first thing in the morning, when the other person is catching up on their mail, dictating letters, planning the morning calls and generally getting their day under way. Last thing at night is equally poor, as people, not unnaturally, resent being delayed in the office by somebody trying to pitch to them.

Always ask: 'Is this a good time to talk briefly, or should I call you back?'

Not only does such a question demonstrate courtesy and consideration, but it can actually give you an opening to make a call which is bound to get past the switchboard, receptionist, secretary, personal assistant and all the other armies of employees that senior management use to safeguard their privacy.

Use the technique of offering a specific time for the call should the person say they cannot talk at that moment: 'I understand, would 10.15 be more suitable?' If this is agreed, the next time you call you can honestly inform anyone who questions your right to speak to their boss: 'He asked me to ring him at this time.'

3. Use AIDA

AIDA stands for the four key elements of all successful sales calls, especially cold calling (see below).

A stands for *attention*. You must make the caller sit up and take notice of what you have to say, in order to avoid becoming the victim of distracted listening.
I is for *interest*. In order to hold that attention the message must satisfy the WIIFM ('What's in it for me?') factor. Remember – people are most interested in *themselves*!
D reminds us that, before anything can be sold it is first necessary to create a *desire* in the prospect's mind.
A is for *action*. The call should end with some clearly defined activity.

Before dialling the number have a clear idea of what you hope to achieve. Always ask yourself, 'What is my purpose in making this call?'

If attempting to arrange an appointment, where refusal to meet you at all is a possibility, have alternative times and dates in mind.

By asking, 'Would 10 o'clock on Friday 23rd be convenient?', you direct the other person's attention to whether he, or she, is free at that time instead of wondering whether they want to meet you in the first place.

4. Stand Up to Sound More Authoritative . . .

Telephoning while standing, literally, heightens your sense of authority while sharpening your mind. When standing our whole system becomes more aroused and alert.

5. Try Changing Ears

Bizarre as this may sound, research into what psychologists term dichotic listening (where a verbal message arrives at only one ear) suggests that the ear used to hear the call may influence the way that communication is interpreted.

Medical investigators have established that, in the vast majority of right-handed people, the chief language centres are in the left hemisphere of the brain. It is here, in two main areas, that verbal messages are interpreted and constructed.

Research shows the left side of the brain is specialised for logical reasoning. It is here, for instance, that tasks such as mathematics and analytical thinking occur.

The right hemisphere, by contrast, tends to perform more intuitive activities, such as fantasising and imagining.

When a sound is received only, for instance, in the right ear the messages are transmitted to both the left and right sides of the brain. However, transmission rates between ears and the two sides of the brain are not identical, with signals reaching the opposite (left) hemisphere fractionally ahead of that on the same side (right) as the ear. Although extremely small, this difference appears to affect the way in which information is processed.

Just as we favour a particular hand, foot or eye (to discover your dominant eye, imagine sighting a rifle or looking through a telescope. The eye you leave open is dominant), we also have a preferred ear. This can make ear swopping a bit uncomfortable at first and using the right ear is a problem for right-handed people who have to take notes during a call. Despite these problems, you might find it helpful to try the following strategy.

Take factual calls using your right ear

It could help you analyse the information being given in a more objective manner. This may make it easier to spot logical inconsistencies or errors of fact.

Right ear listening is especially helpful when getting an accurate grasp on the facts and figures of a proposal is of prime importance.

Take emotional calls using your left ear

Studies indicate that the best way of dealing with more emotional issues, which demand intuition rather than ruthless logic, is to place the phone against your *left* ear. This increases sensitivity to unspoken feelings and enhances empathy. Try it and see whether this works for you.

6. Dealing with Difficult Calls

There are some calls we all dread receiving – or making. Many people, for instance, hate having to reprimand or criticise others. While nothing can turn a tough call into a pleasant one, try these practical ways of making life a little easier.

- Whenever possible take the initiative and make the call. You'll be able to prepare your remarks rather than being caught unawares.
- Get quickly to the point. Do not try to soften the blow by skirting around the problem. Say something like, 'My reason for calling is. . .' then launch right into it.
- If caught unawares by a critical call never respond immediately. Make an excuse and return the call when you have thought through your answers.
- Use your knowledge of personalities when planning your response. Counter **scientists** with facts, appeal to the emotions of **mediators**, work on a **go-getter's** desire for status and take advantage of a **dynamo's** low threshold of boredom.

7. Plug into the Personality Types

Use your knowledge of the personality types, described above, when planning your call.

When talking to the **scientist** quote firm evidence, preferably statistical, in support of your claims.

Appeal to the emotions of people-oriented **mediators**.

Work on the **go-getter's** motivation towards status and leadership.

Take advantage of the **dynamo's** desire for enthusiasm, variety and change.

8. Reading Others Right

Disraeli once remarked that there was 'no index of character so sure as the voice'. To listen empathically use that index of character to gain an insight into how the other person sees a particular situation. Although this is never easy, here are some practical ways to reduce guesswork.

- Never rely on voice quality alone. There are too many unknowns for your logical left brain to work with. Instead, rely on your intuitive right brain.

  As you listen, remain relaxed and allow an impression of the speaker to form slowly in your mind. These unforced impressions are often remarkably accurate.
- A fast speaking rate – provided the content makes good sense – is correlated with above average intelligence. Someone who talks quickly usually thinks quickly.
- Hesitations, stammering and pauses often betray areas of anxiety or indecision.
- Depending on context, unusual emphasis on certain words may betray subconscious like or dislike.

9. Create a Caller Fact File

A universal rule of human relationships is, other things being equal, we like best those who seem to like us best. To like somebody is to know them.

By communicating a positive, sincere interest in the other person you can develop that sense of friendship on which consumer loyalty is based.

As you glean information through chatting, make a note of it, either using an index card system (using the format suggested below) or directly on to a computer (but bear in mind the Data Protection Act).

10. Be Polite – Say Thanks

Always make 'thank you' calls whenever you've received co-operation. If, for example, a company mails you information about itself as requested, be sure to call the employee concerned to acknowledge receipt and thank them. This is not only courteous, it can also be a great way of developing a friend on the inside who will provide additional information or leads.

Quick and easy to make, such calls work wonders for future co-operation. But never delay your thanks. The closer they are to the action which pleased you the more powerful their effect.

Phoning customers when *not* trying to pitch to them – provided you don't choose a busy time or ramble on – is a great way of building up a relationship.

Once they look on you as a friend and ally repeat orders are a cinch.

11. Saying Goodbye

Ending a call efficiently is no less important than starting one correctly. Chatter on too long and you risk confusing, boring or irritating the other person. For a satisfactory conclusion use the P–F–G strategy.

- Be **polite.** When dealing with a relative stranger use their name in your final sentence. If there are some facts you particularly want remembered, repeat them immediately prior to saying goodbye. The way memory works means we recall best the things heard first and last in a conversation.

- Be **Firm.** Avoid being diverted into an irrelevant discussion. If you find this hard to do have a few plausible excuses such as 'Sorry, I'm wanted on the other phone' as a standby tactic. Usually, however, if your tone is positive the other person will get the message. Having said farewell . . .
- Be **gone.** Replace the receiver and start thinking about the next call you want to make.

12. Dealing with Answering Machines

If you run, or deal with, one-person or small businesses, the chances are you'll find yourself talking to, or trying to persuade others to talk to, an answering machine.

In theory these gadgets should be a boon to the one-person business, ensuring that important calls and potential prospects are never lost to the opposition. In practice answering machines can prove a barrier to business.

There are five main fears which make it difficult for some people to get the best out of answering machines.

Technophobia

Many people are irrationally fearful of all types of technology. For them interacting with any type of machine is painful and having to talk to a gadget makes them highly anxious. You can tell technophobes by the messages left on your machines: 'Hello, Oh God don't tell me I'm talking to a machine . . . Oh . . . Oh . . . call me back.'

Since they seldom leave a name or phone number their call is rarely returned, thus deepening their fear and loathing of the answer machine.

Help yourself by planning your message carefully. When caught unawares by a machine, ring off, work out what you want to say – maybe writing down key points – then redial. Be sure to give your name, phone number, state briefly the purpose of your call, and include time and date of the message.

When preparing an out-going message (OGM) for your own answering machine, make certain it is clear yet sufficiently comprehensive to ensure you get all the information needed. If, for instance, your machine only allows a brief message to be left then make this clear on your OGM.

Your voice should sound warm, affable and welcoming. Check for user friendliness by calling your own line from another phone. Ask yourself whether, if you heard that message, you'd be most likely to leave a message or hastily replace the handset.

Fear of sounding inarticulate

Many people take time to get into the swing of a conversation. They have to warm themselves up with some casual chit-chat before getting around to the main purpose of their call. The answering machine makes them fearful because it inhibits this preliminary warm-up.

Help yourself by keeping the message short and always including an action you want taken, such as being called back.

Fear of running out of time

Knowing that a tape is unwinding worries some people. They are afraid they will run out of time before saying all they need and want to say. This causes them to forget the key points in their message. Hence the need to plan, and perhaps even write down, what you want to say – at least until you have become accustomed to using the answerphone.

Help yourself by using the suggestions above. In addition, forget that you are speaking to a machine and imagine the person you wanted to talk to is listening at the other end.

Fear of being recorded

Some people feel anxious that their slips and mistakes will be on tape and can be played back to anybody.

Help yourself by giving yourself positive feedback after leaving a message. Notice all the good things which you did. If anything about the way you dealt with the answerphone was unsatisfactory in your view, then identify the problem and work out a better way of responding next time around.

If you own an answering machine analyse the way other people leave messages. Use any good features of their approach and avoid the mistakes they make.

Fear of making mistakes

This is especially likely in people who need to be assured that their facts and figures are fully understood. They usually prefer the immediate feedback of a personal chat because it allows them to probe for misconceptions or misunderstandings – 'Are you sure you understand that?' – and to provide instant correction of errors. Left with an answering machine they worry about ambiguities distorting the message.

Help yourself by keeping the message as short as possible. Spell any tricky words – using Alpha/Bravo code – where appropriate. For instance, to give the postcode AC20 0BY it may be better to say A for Alpha; C for Charlie; 20; zero; B for Bravo; Y for Yankee. Repeat numbers, dates, times etc.

Always Do Your Homework Before Calling

Before making a call to a prospective customer complete the entries on your telephone information card (see Action Plan 8 below).

Essential details include the name and address of the company, their phone number and the extension of the person you want to call together with his, or her, name – the correct pronunciation if this is unusual or difficult – and their position in the company.

Such information can often be obtained from reference books or company publications. Failing that, make a separate call to obtain this information.

Knowing exactly to whom you wish to speak is the fastest way of getting through the outer defences of receptionists and secretaries, which most senior executives use to protect their time and privacy. Yet these are the people you need to talk to in order to make the call worth while.

Keep your telephone information card beside you as you make the call and complete the additional entries immediately after completing it. Use the reverse of this card to note down any action taken.

Three Golden Rules for Cold Calls

When researching follow these rules.

- **Be brief.** People are busy; they haven't either the time or the inclination to listen to a long, rambling sales presentation or request for information.
- **Be positive** about what you are selling or seeking.
- **Be polite.** Even if the response you get is irritating, never let your annoyance show.

Should I Use a Script?

Carefully prepared scripts can be helpful when cold calling and are much used in telemarketing. But when seeking research information or arranging for a first meeting my view is that it is best to use them only as a general guide or memory aid to remind you of the key facts you want to discover.

Seven Mistakes that Weaken Phone Power

Here are seven mistakes to avoid and ways of recovering from them should you slip.

Mistake one: Getting the person's name wrong
Here you can only apologise and make certain you use the name correctly from then on.

When given a name for the first time impress it on to your memory through silent repetition and frequent use.

After the call ends, note down the person's name, together with any other personal information given during the conversation, such as names and ages of children. File this information carefully. It will help you develop an even warmer relationship during later calls.

Always have your telephone information card by you when making the call and correct your spelling if this was wrong. When it's a hard name to pronounce, write down the word phonetically as well.

Mistake two: Rambling on
If you catch yourself doing this, don't stop dead. Briefly recap the key points of your ramble.

Mistake three: Introducing irrelevant information
Avoid this by planning. If you fall into the trap then make a mental note not to do it again. Don't apologise because you'll simply draw attention to something the other person may not, up to that moment, have noticed.

Mistake four: Pretending to knowledge you don't have
If you are caught out in this, embarrassment is almost bound to follow. All you can do is thank the speaker courteously for pointing out your error.

Mistake five: Offering too many alternative times and dates for an appointment
It simply confuses the issue and distracts the other from making a decision.

Mistake six: Sounding too eager
If you come over as too enthusiastic you'll sound either amateurish or desperate. At worst this can cost you the business and at best place you in a very weak negotiating position. Bear in mind that the benefits you are offering, when worth while, will significantly assist the other company to make or save money. If you feel that your opening comments sounded too eager, correct this by turning down the first appointment offered. This is not usually risky. If they really want to see you, they'll find an alternative slot.

Mistake seven: Not confirming the time and date during the call
Recover by phoning that person, or their secretary, the day before the meeting to confirm.

Making Your Telephone a Company Ambassador

More than 95 per cent of your company's daily visitors come via the telephone. How they are treated on arrival can have a dramatic impact on their desire to do business with you, whether it's for the first time or for repeat orders. Unfortunately many are left with the impression of a surly, inefficient, poorly managed business for whom customers are not the life-blood but an irritating inconvenience.

We have all had the experience of turning up at a company to be greeted by the corporate Rotweiler who barks out curt instructions and leave you feeling apologetic for daring even to enter the building.

It's the same over the phone. First impressions really do

count and business can be lost before it reaches your sales team if those impressions are bad ones.

Ten Commandments for Answering Calls

1. Your telephone should never be allowed to ring more than three times before being answered.

   If it does you'll lose customers who can't be bothered to hang on for your convenience and create a negative image among those patient enough to wait.

2. Everybody in the office should take responsibility for answering a ringing phone. This means training staff in good telephone technique, and providing them with sufficient knowledge about the organisation to deal with enquiries efficiently and speedily.

   They must know who should be contacted for any particular caller and how to put them through to the correct extension.

   There should be a specific procedure for the taking and passing on of messages. Staff should know what details are required if the person is to be called back. Return numbers should always be taken.

3. The telephone should always be answered as follows: 'Good/morning/afternoon/evening, this is [give number or name of company, or both], [name of person answering] here, how can I help you?'

   The structure of this response is important.

   Starting with a good morning etc. is not merely polite, but allows the other person to direct their attention back to the call.

   While waiting for the receiver to be picked up, even

if it has been answered within the required three rings, the caller's mind tends to wander. As a result they usually fail to attend to the first second or so of the response.

If you immediately answer with the number or company name, the caller may not be fully attentive and could get confused or ask you to repeat it. Either wastes time – yours and theirs – and is easily avoided.

Identifying the company and/or number is clearly important to reassure the caller they have dialled correctly or, if it is a wrong number, to establish this fact promptly in order not to waste time.

Finally, giving the person your name establishes a positive relationship right from the start. It makes you, and your organisation, sound welcoming and friendly.

4. Never answer the telephone while eating or drinking, or in the middle of a conversation with someone else in your office.

5. Never put one hand over the phone to speak to someone nearby; it makes your organization sound small and unprofessional.

6. If you promise to phone back then do so. Few things are more calculated to annoy prospective customers than messages which remain unanswered.

7. If you don't know the answer to a question or problem then admit as much and promise to return their call with the correct information either personally or by contacting the appropriate employee within your organisation.

8. Check the key points of your conversation using Reflective Listening. This prevents unnecessary and possibly costly blunders.

9. Always thank the caller for taking the trouble to ring.

10. Always allow the caller to hang up first. If you put down the phone first and their line goes dead it ends the call on an unfriendly note.

ACTION PLAN 8

Copy the following details on to index cards and keep one by you whenever you are making a call.

Caller Fact File

Type of prospect approached [i.e. vendors or people you buy from; business people you have met; friends and acquaintances; previous job associates; people who have responded to advertising etc.]

Date compiled:
Phone number and extension:
Fax number:
Date phoned:
Personal details:
Remarks:
Results and/or follow-up:

Complete these cards immediately your call ends. Include any personal details obtained during the conversation, for instance names and ages of children, hobbies, interests, likes and dislikes.

Do they have a dog? If it was mentioned in a telephone call, that dog is likely to be important to them, so keep a record of its name, breed and gender.

Are they just going on holiday? If so, note it down and be sure to enquire how they enjoyed the break on a subsequent call.

Used judiciously, personal information of this kind significantly increases the speed with which you can develop a close working relationship.

KEY POINTS

- When used correctly the telephone is a powerful sales tool.
- You can often identify how a person likes to be talked and sold to in business by the way he or she uses language.
- Stand up when making a tricky call to give yourself more confidence.
- Relax prior to making anxiety-arousing calls.
- Smile when speaking and imagine yourself talking to a living person rather than a disembodied voice down the line. You may find it helpful to keep a photograph of the person in front of you or conjure up the features of a stranger from the sound of their voice.
- Try using your left ear for calls which require an intuitive approach and your right ear for those which need objective analysis.

STAGE THREE

Preparing Your Sales Presentation

'BE SELECTIVE. BE CONCISE. Don't tell people what you know; tell them what they need to know, what it means and why it matters.'

General David Jones

'MAKING THE SIMPLE COMPLICATED is commonplace; making the complicated simple, awesomely simple, that's creativity.'

Charles Mingus (1922–79), American jazz musician and singer

SELLING VERSUS SHELVING

'JUST LISTENING will not get you much these days. You've got to help customers feel the impact of your listening.'

David H. Radack

BEFORE WE can consider the challenge of creating powerfully persuasive sales presentations, we need to be clear on a basic point.

What does the word *selling* really mean?

What is the salesperson actually trying to achieve through the process of making a sale?

Before reading any further you might like to write down your own definition below.

My definition of selling is ....

....

....

The *Concise Oxford Dictionary* defines a sale as 'the exchange of a commodity for money etc.'. Maybe your own definition is along similar lines.

While this definition is obviously accurate, so far as it goes, I would argue that it is unhelpful as the basis for putting together an effective sales presentation. The problem is that it fails to identify the single most vital aspect of successful selling.

A sales feature so crucial that you cannot hope to win new business without appreciating its importance.

That is the concept of bringing about changes in the thoughts and actions of your prospective customer.

Winning new business always implies such a change in another person's ideas, opinions, feelings, attitudes, beliefs and behaviour. When no such change occurs the transaction is more usefully and appropriately described not as selling but as *shelving*.

An example will help to make this vital distinction clear.

A Tale of Two Retailers

Not long ago my brother visited a photographic dealer to buy some rolls of colour film for use on a holiday overseas. He asked for six rolls of film which the assistant located on the shelf, handed to him and then took payment. He left the shop a couple of minutes after entering it.

Was that a sale?

Clearly the compilers of the *Oxford Dictionary* would claim that it was. A commodity had been exchanged for money. Perhaps you agree with them.

But now let us consider a very different scenario. Imagine what might have happened if, instead of immediately giving him the film, the assistant had engaged my brother in a friendly conversation.

He could have discussed his photographic requirements and listened attentively while my brother talked about his holiday. He might then have offered to check the camera free of charge, pointing out that it would be a shame to lose irreplaceable holiday memories through faulty photographic equipment.

Having examined the camera he could have remarked that being a fairly basic model it could not be guaranteed to produce top quality results under all lighting conditions.

He would then have demonstrated the latest version, explained its benefits and illustrated them with attractive photographs before offering my brother a trade-in against his present camera.

Persuaded by this presentation my brother could well have decided to buy a new camera for his holiday. After all, what's the cost of a camera set against the possible disappointment of lost holiday snaps?

In this case, it is clear that the assistant initiated the following changes in my brother's thoughts and behaviour.

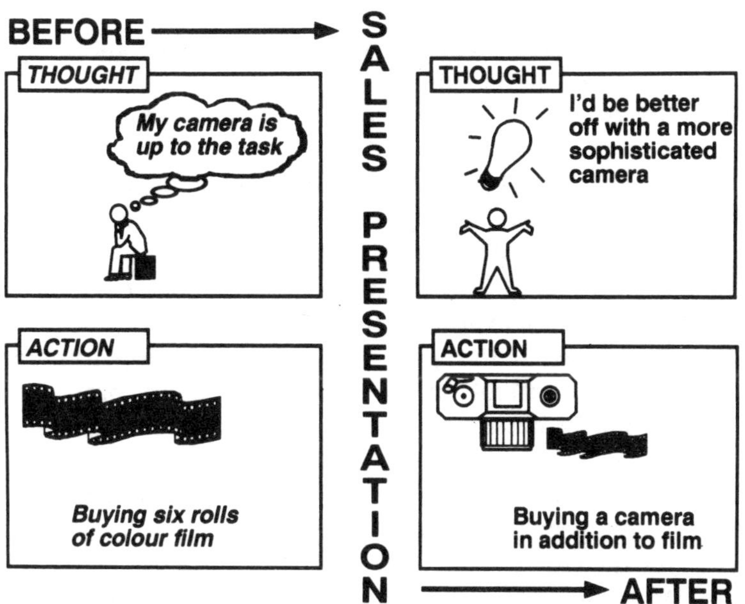

The sales assistant takes the film requested off the shelf, hands it across the counter and accepts payment.

That is shelving.

The retailer has made no attempt to change buying behaviour.

The sales assistant uses communications skills to bring about a change in buying behaviour.

That is selling.

In fact my definition of a sale is: 'The active initiation of change'.

The purpose of all sales presentations is actively to initiate change.

Shelving means servicing an existing customer.

Selling means winning new business.

While *shelving* may, for a while, meet the needs and expectations of established customers, it cannot, by definition, gain you additional customers, since this *always* involves one or more of four changes.

A new customer will have done the following.

- **Change supplier**. They have awarded you their business in place of a regular supplier.
- **Changed methods of working**. They have accepted a need for new equipment and/or services. For example, changing from typewriters to word processors.
- **Changed price**. They agree to buy a superior product or service instead of the lower cost ones currently being used. For example, by upgrading to a faster computer system or buying a more expensive company car.
- **Changed their philosophy**. A customer is persuaded to adopt a different outlook on how business should be done. For example, by outsourcing work previously done in-house.

Recognising that winning new business *always* involves some type of change makes it easier to understand, and overcome, sales resistance.

When customers say 'no' to the goods or services you are

offering, what they may really be rejecting is the threat posed by change.

For many years IBM cleverly exploited such insecurity with an advertising slogan which said: 'Nobody ever got fired for buying IBM.' Logic may have persuaded the would-be purchasers that IBM computers would increase efficiency. The reassuring message helped overcome emotional resistance caused by a reluctance to change. Later a rival firm slyly counter-attacked by adding '. . . but they never got promoted either.' The suggestion that only their computers could advance a manager's career prospects cleverly transformed the previously reassuring message into a slightly threatening one.

When pitching for new business it is essential to keep this key concept of initiating change at the top of your mind.

Every sales presentation should have but one purpose. And that is to make the idea of change appear not only highly beneficial but also reassuringly easy and straightforward.

Change is Often Seen as a Threat

Many people regard change more as a threat than an opportunity. Not surprisingly, therefore, they dislike it, distrust it and seek to avoid it. A majority of us would probably agree with Ogden Nash's view that 'progress might have been all right once, but it's gone on far too long!'

As a result the prospect of changing triggers powerful psychological defences which create a major barrier to sales success.

Even when logic tells us that change is normal and inevitable, our gut reaction is often to oppose it, to wish it had happened earlier, or later, or not at all.

Since change is typically viewed as threatening our

security and happiness, it's not surprising that we so dislike it, distrust it, fear it and seek to avoid it.

Nor is it remarkable that even the contemplation of changing arouses considerable anxiety, which we frequently deal with in one of two ways:

- avoidance; or
- denial.

Although both can lead to a refusal to buy, the underlying causes of such sales resistance differ and must be countered in different ways.

Sales Resistance Caused by Avoidance

Customers who are seeking to reduce their anxiety through avoidance recognise changes are needed but still refuse to do anything about them.

They hesitate, procrastinate, hold endless meetings, demand more and more information, seek constant reassurance, and will tell you 'I know what you are saying makes sense.

'It's true we ought to update that equipment. I am sure our staff would benefit from this training programme. But I don't know. I'm not sure the time is right.

'Maybe if you were to come back next year . . . I tell you what, I'll think about it!'

Since the time is somehow never right, no sale will normally be made unless changing circumstances force change on the purchaser.

Chronic avoiders often operate in what I referred to earlier as a 'Yes but . . .' culture.

THE UNALIGNED "YES - BUT" CULTURE

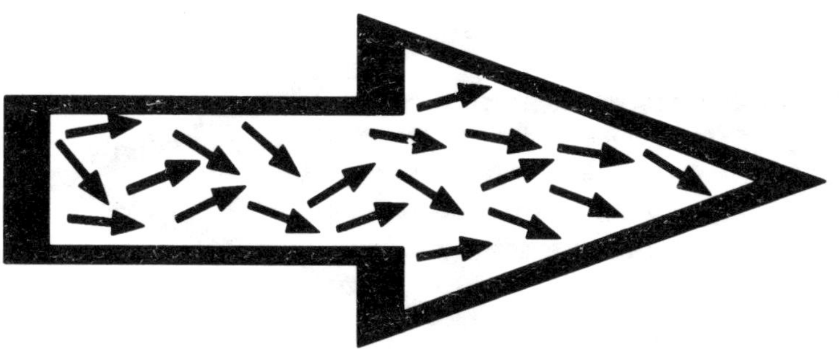

Such companies are rarely successful and often trapped on the plateau or *stagnation* phase of development described in Stage Two. People within them pull in different directions and everybody is running scared of making a mistake which means, of course, that they seldom make a decision.

Whenever anybody comes up with a suggestion that involves change, their anxiety immediately leads them to counter it with 'Yes but . . .'

> 'We've always done it that way.'
> 'The unions won't wear it.'
> 'My department chief wouldn't accept it.'
> 'We don't have the budget for it.'

This contrasts with the gung-ho, go-ahead, change welcoming atmosphere of most start-ups and high achieving, mature companies where a 'Yes and . . .' culture dominates.

THE ALIGNED "YES AND......" CULTURE

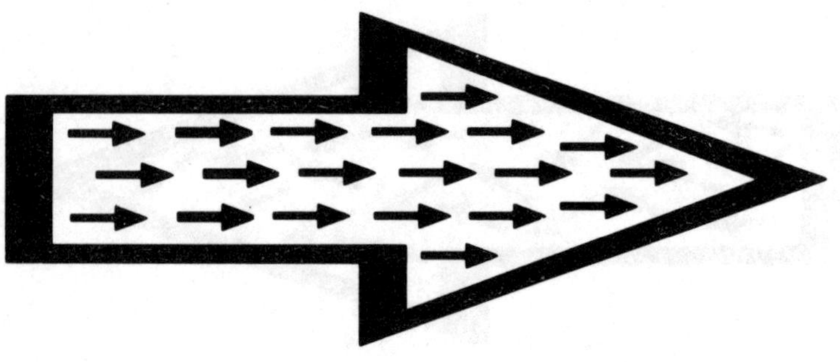

Their response to the challenge of change, from whatever source or direction it comes, is to say 'Yes and . . .'

> 'We could use the new system to produce greater revenue.'
> 'If modified to our special needs that will cut our overheads.'

In other words they see the potential of a new idea, and have both the creative ability and courage to take it on board.

Such an attitude is not the consequence but the cause of their success.

When confronted by sales resistance caused by avoidance, the purpose of your sales presentation should be to make the necessity for immediate change appear not only essential, but the least emotionally threatening optio available.

Sales Resistance Due to Denial

Denial, which functions at a deeper psychological level, prevents customers from even recognising that change is needed in the first place.

Selling to a customer in deep denial is virtually impossible unless you are able to penetrate the armour of their psychological defences by adopting exactly the right sales presentation.

Here, your purpose must be twofold.

First you have to remove the client's mental blindfold so they directly confront the need for change. Next you must prevent the client moving out of denial and into avoidance by providing reassurance as to the ease with which that change can be effected.

STICKY MOMENTS WITH VELCRO

William Kessler is manager of the transportation division of Velcro USA Inc. and a truly world-class salesman.

While most people think of Velcro as a clothing item its main market is in motor and aircraft manufacture. Bill had flown to Europe to meet the chief engineer of an automobile manufacturer.

'We have no need for your product,' was this man's greeting.

'Fine,' Bill replied. He shut his briefcase and prepared to leave. The engineer was stunned.

'You've flown all the way from America just to see me,' he protested. 'Aren't you going to try harder for an order?'

'No point,' Bill replied. 'If you don't use Velcro you'll either go broke, and why should we want to do business with a company heading for bankruptcy? Or you'll be taken over by a Japanese company. We already do business with all of them anyhow.'

'Hmmm,' said the engineer, emerging swiftly from denial. 'Perhaps we should start again.'

'Sure,' Bill agreed amiably. He held out his hand. 'Hi, my name is William Kessler, and I'm from Velcro . . .'

A substantial order followed!

Lesson: People will often agree to buy when convinced there is a valid reason for your not selling to them. Known as 'closing the bag', this technique can effectively persuade a client in denial to accept reality. But it is a strategy that must be used with care and skill.

Avoidance and Denial Can Provide the Basis for Long-Term Success

Although initially challenging, prospects who start out by avoiding and denying the need for changes can be transformed into excellent long-term customers.

Once you have relieved their anxiety and helped them through the trauma of change, the powerful emotions generated cause them to forge a deep emotional commitment with the supplier who supported and encouraged them. It's the same type of psychological bond one finds between people rescued from some disaster and those responsible for saving their lives.

This makes it far easier for you to become a trusted partner and friend rather than somebody your customer just does business with. But be very careful. Emotionally vulnerable people who feel betrayed or let down by their vendors can become equally vehement in their criticism.

Salespeople who persuade avoiding or denying customers to accept change must do their best to ensure that their trust is never abused or taken for granted. Do this and you will have won not only new business but a client for life.

Making Sales also Involves Change

The same fear of change makes it hard for some people to confront the challenge of winning new business. Most of us are brought up to seek and value the approval of others.

This need to be held in high, positive regard becomes a part of our self-image through a process psychologists call *internalisation.*

Because rejection threatens self-esteem, the majority of people strive to avoid it. Selling means facing a significant amount of rejection. The psychological stress and distress this creates is a major reason why so many of those who embark on a sales career give up within the first few months. They are only going to become sales professionals provided they can tolerate those rejections long enough to develop an objective attitude towards such unavoidable rebuffs.

People who lack this professional training and yet are obliged to pitch for new business may become extremely stressed by refusals, no matter how politely those turn-downs are phrased. This occurs because every rejection threatens their self-image, so undermining confidence and esteem. Like reluctant prospects they too safeguard themselves against this perceived threat by taking refuge in avoidance or denial.

They are unwilling to make telephone sales calls, especially when these involve cold calling.

Having arranged a sales meeting they fail to close the deal correctly. If rejected once their confidence fails them and they never go back. They may refuse to accept that without actively seeking out new business their own will go under.

'Something will turn up', they tell you with Micawber-like optimism as they plunge ever deeper into debt and denial.

In Stage Four I shall be offering practical techniques for

overcoming the mental and physical barriers this negative attitude creates.

BEATING DOORKNOB PHOBIA

The following advice is given by Arthur Priebe, one of the world's great insurance salesmen to help salespeople overcome their fear of rejection. When afflicted by doorknob phobia hold the following conversation with yourself.

'Where am I now?'

'Waiting in the lobby.'

'Where do I want to be?'

'In the customer's office'

'What's the worst thing that can happen if I go in to see him?'

'He'll throw me out into the lobby.'

'Well, since that's where I am now how can I be any worse off?'

Lesson: Talk yourself into, not out of, confronting the challenges of winning new business.

ACTION PLAN 9

DEVELOP A VISION FOR YOURSELF AND YOUR COMPANY

Visions imply changes in the established order. This is why business visionaries are over-represented among entrepreneurs and why, like Lee Iacocca, the saviour of Chrysler, they are indispensable when an organisation gets into difficulties.

Visions must always be expressed as concrete and realistic goals in order to be accomplished. The more concisely you can express your goals, the more likely you are to achieve them.

To help focus your thoughts on short, medium and long-term visions, write down your chief sales goals in the spaces below. Make this a regular exercise, modifying, expanding and updating goals to keep pace with changing circumstances.

My major sales goal for the next twelve months is:

....

My major sales goal for the next two years is:

....

My major sales goal for the next five years is:

....

Rule: Where you stand at present matters far less than where you're headed.

NEVER SAY 'CAN'T'

This word produces an absolute block to sales attainment. 'I can't do this ...', 'We can't achieve that...'.

For people who say 'can't' the world becomes filled with impossibilities. Contrast that negative belief with the positive yet realistic statement, 'I don't know ...'.

Those who say 'don't' instead of 'can't' fill their world with possibilities.

'We don't know how to do this ... but we will find out.'
'I don't know how to achieve that ... but I will learn.'

Have you got into the habit of, almost automatically, thinking or saying 'can't' when the chance for change presents itself?

If you are unsure use the record below to count the can'ts you use over the next two days.

Just cross through a CAN'T (from those set out below) as soon as possible after the word has been thought or uttered – there are fifty of them which should be sufficient for even the most negative person!

This exercise in itself will help remind you to think 'don't' not 'can't' in future.

CAN'T	CAN'T	CAN'T	CAN'T	CAN'T
CAN'T	CAN'T	CAN'T	CAN'T	CAN'T
CAN'T	CAN'T	CAN'T	CAN'T	CAN'T
CAN'T	CAN'T	CAN'T	CAN'T	CAN'T
CAN'T	CAN'T	CAN'T	CAN'T	CAN'T
CAN'T	CAN'T	CAN'T	CAN'T	CAN'T
CAN'T	CAN'T	CAN'T	CAN'T	CAN'T
CAN'T	CAN'T	CAN'T	CAN'T	CAN'T
CAN'T	CAN'T	CAN'T	CAN'T	CAN'T
CAN'T	CAN'T	CAN'T	CAN'T	CAN'T

If a stronger lesson is needed to break the habit, place an elastic band on your wrist and snap it every time the 'c' word comes to your mind or your mouth.

Rule: They have half the deed done who have made a beginning.

BE ACTION ORIENTATED

Actively seek ways of finding and winning new business.

Pick up the telephone and make those sales calls.

Write those sales letters.

Research new contracts. Arrange meetings with potential customers.

Determine what needs to be done and then DO IT.

Remember the Law of Multiple Effect and become action orientated. Start sales moving, no matter how slowly at first and you'll find that winning new business quickly gathers momentum.

If you wait for something to turn up, you'll spend your whole life staring at your toes.

KEY POINTS

- Selling always involves the active initiation of change. Everything else is shelving.
- Winning new business is about changing the mind-set and behaviour of a prospective customer.
- Change makes people feel anxious. Anxiety leads to avoidance and denial, defence mechanisms responsible for a great deal of sales resistance.
- The purpose of a sales presentation is to persuade people to welcome the changes you propose, and to see them as an opportunity for advancement rather than a threat.
- Once converted to accepting a change which proves ultimately successful, the emotional bond forged can keep customers loyal for life.

8 THE MAGIC BULLET OF COMMUNICATIONS

'SAMSON slew ten thousand Philistines with the jaw-bone of an ass, and every day thousands of orders are killed in the same way.'

Bert Schlain

BACK IN the sixteenth century Francis Bacon commented, 'Knowledge itself is power.' What he actually wrote was '*Nam et ipsa scientia potestas est*', which makes perfect sense if you speak Latin and no sense at all if you do not.

This raises the single most important element of a successful sales presentation, which is that the message be communicated in a language your intended audience clearly understands.

This may sound so obvious it scarcely merits stating, yet every day new business is lost because the sales presentation is insufficiently comprehensible to those at whom it is aimed. This occurs for three main reasons.

- **The language is too complex**, filled with jargon or pitched at a level of technical expertise beyond that of your intended audience.

  Teachers and university lecturers may not seem like salespersons but that is, in fact, what they are. Specialists selling, or attempting to sell, knowledge about and an interest in their particular subject to students.

  When those lessons and lectures are pitched at a level of understanding far greater than that possessed by their listeners, bafflement and boredom are the inevitable consequences.
- **The language is too simplistic**. The exact opposite of the first barrier, this occurs when a presentation patronises an audience by underestimating their knowledge.
- **The delivery is incomprehensible**. This happens when the message is communicated too softly or too rapidly, when the speaker swallows his or her words or has a strong regional accent unfamiliar to the audience.

Clarity of Purpose

When preparing any communication you have to ensure that it is easily and fully comprehensible to those at whom your message is aimed. When preparing the specialist form of communication, termed a sales presentation, this will only be achieved provided two basic considerations are kept in mind:

- the time available;
- the level of understanding and knowledge possessed by your audience. A communication which appeals to a specialist may baffle the non-expert, while a message that makes good sense to the layperson could appear patronisingly self-evident to the professional.

These two factors determine both content and style of presentation.

When constructing your presentation, therefore, keep these six questions in the forefront of your mind.

1. What is the purpose of this presentation – what do I want it to accomplish?
2. What does my audience need to know in order that this purpose is achieved?
3. What knowledge do they possess?
4. How much background information is necessary?
5. What time constraints are there?
6. What physical barriers exist (i.e. language problems)?

The Magic Bullet Theory of Communications

Before looking at the nuts and bolts of creating such a presentation, it will be useful to step back slightly and consider what we actually mean by communication.

One widely used technical definition states that it is: 'A process whereby a source transmits a message through some channel to a receiver.' To this is usually added 'with feedback', taking into account the fact that audiences will always respond in some way, either verbally or non-verbally, or both, and that this feedback may be favourable or unfavourable.

Immediate feedback significantly modifies both the content and delivery of a speaker. An experienced salesperson who observes resistance to his or her proposals in the prospect's body language, for example, will adjust the presentation accordingly.

The inexperienced salesperson, by contrast, may press on regardless, insensitive to such negative feedback, and will probably lose their sale as a result.

COMMUNICATION CHANNELS IN A SALES PRESENTATION

VISUAL = EXPRESSION
GESTURE
POSTURE

MATCH/MISMATCH WITH VERBAL INFORMATION

AUDITORY = WORDS USED
VOICE TONE
SPEED OF DELIVERY
ACCENT/DIALECT

MATCH/MISMATCH WITH VISUAL INFORMATION

THE CASE OF THE ONE-LEGGED LECTURER

A group of first-year psychology students decided to put their knowledge of what feedback conditioning was into practice, by forcing their professor to lecture while standing on one leg. The students had learned that any behaviour promptly rewarded is likely to be repeated. They had also noticed their lecturer was in the habit of occasionally rubbing his right foot against his left leg. Accordingly they showed interest by giving him eye-contact, nodding and smiling only when he was doing so. As soon as he stopped they appeared bored.

Before long, so the story goes, the professor gave all his lectures standing on one leg without realising why.

Lesson: Body language is a powerful way of manipulating a prospect's behaviour (see Stage Four).

The definition given above is sometimes called the 'magic bullet theory of communications', since the underlying assumption is that information is fired from one person's brain into the brain of another to create a desired effect. This implies a cause – effect relationship between the communication and its consequences.

While this may seem reasonable in theory, as everyone who sells knows to their cost, it seldom works out that way in real life because:

- your magic bullet fails to hit the target;

- your audience is hit fair and square then fails to fall over as expected;
- your gun misfires;
- your magic bullet misses the target entirely!

Put simply, there's many a slip between ear and lip.

How Problems Arise

Messages may contain mistakes

Not long ago my brother received a letter from the headmaster of his son's school, regretting that due to increasing costs it was necessary to raise the school fees which, from the following term, would be '£4,000 per anum'! My brother replied that if it was all the same to the headmaster he would prefer to pay as he had always done, through the nose!

That single missing 'n' had transformed the meaning of the headmaster's communication.

Messages may contain ambiguities

Because language is sometimes not very precise, a communication can be interpreted in a way not intended by the sender.

Consider the sales presentation to which we are most exposed, the television commercial. The pictures we see and the sounds we hear have been crafted by some of the most experienced and creative minds in marketing. Every shot, every image within those shots, every edit, every full stop, comma, sales point, product presentation, invitation, exhortation and explanation has been thought about, argued over, discussed, rewritten, designed and redesigned dozens, perhaps hundreds, of times in an effort to ensure maximum impact.

Often more than a million pounds and thousands of hours have gone into honing and polishing the final results which appear on your screen. The underlying assumptions have been researched by highly paid consultants; the film itself previewed by audiences whose physical and mental responses have been monitored second by second.

It may well have been shown to so-called focus groups for evaluation and probably tested in just one television region before ever being screened. In short, these are among the most expertly and exactly crafted and delivered sales presentations ever created, which should mean they are clearly and unambiguously understood by their intended audiences. Yet this is not the case.

A 1980 study commissioned by the American Association of Advertising Agencies found nearly every one of the 2,700 viewers surveyed had managed to misunderstand at least some part of the 60 commercials they watched. Overall, misunderstanding amounted to 30 per cent of the total, a level of error which applied to all ages, income levels, education levels and both sexes.

WHEN MARGARET THATCHER WAS NOT AMUSED

A minister in Margaret Thatcher's government recounts how, on one occasion, he received a research document from his department which he considered rubbish.

Never one to suffer fools gladly he scrawled 'balls' across the top by way of comment. Later, realising the document would be seen by the prime minister, he altered this to 'round objects'.

Not long after the file was returned to him with a terse demand from the PM: 'Who is Round and how dare he object!'

Lesson: The exact meaning of a message often lies in the ears and eyes of the receiver.

We add to messages

The meanings we attach to messages represent the sum total of our experiences, social and cultural background, level of education, specialist knowledge, biases, prejudices and our emotional state at the moment the information is received. This means that the same communication presented to a hundred people may be interpreted by them in a hundred subtly different ways. And, if you were to show that message to the same people twenty-four hours later, the meanings might even have changed again.

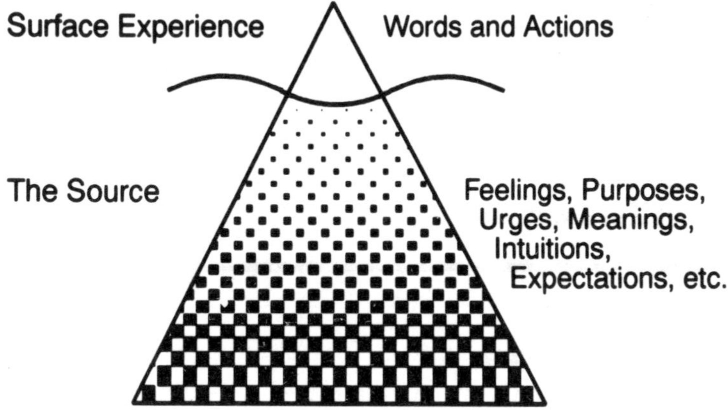

The pyramid of communications shows how every message is interpreted through a complex network of attitudes, beliefs, prejudices, assumptions, ideas, associations, emotions and memories. As a result Pareto's Law often applies to this, as to many other aspects of selling, with 80 per cent of a message being contributed by the receiver.

WHEN TARZAN WAS MISTAKEN FOR JANE

Some years ago, a Minneapolis newspaper published a photograph of a pair of breasts and asked 'Can you identify this famous star?'

In the days following the newspaper published scores of outraged letters from readers accusing them of pornography.

After enjoying their prank for a week, the newspaper printed the whole photograph which showed muscled Tarzan star and former swimming champion Johnny Weismuller! Those breasts were actually his well-developed pectorals!

Lesson: Beliefs not only affect our judgements and behaviour, but distort our interpretation of what we hear and see.

The WIIFM factor

The degree of attention and interest we are willing to invest in such a transaction depends on how personally relevant it seems. In other words we are talking about the WIIFM (What's in it for me?) factor discussed in Stage Two.

And, unless your sales presentation contains a strong element of WIIFM, it will either not be attended to in the first place or heard without being acted upon.

This applies to all audiences, but especially to those made anxious by the prospect of change.

This is becoming ever more important in a world where we are bombarded by information to the point where it is often a case of switch off or burn out.

Surviving Information Overkill

The pioneering psychologist William James once called the world of the newborn baby a 'booming, buzzing confusion'. He might just as well have been describing the modern world of information overkill.

During our every waking moment we are bombarded by information. It's been estimated that 10,000 potential sensory impressions per second, or 288 million per working day, clamour for our attention. Each day we are exposed to hundreds of sales presentations in the form of advertisements on television and on radio, on billboards, hoardings, cereal packets, and supermarket walls, fly-posted on windows of empty shops, carried aloft in balloons, trailed behind aircraft, emblazoned on sportspeople's shirts, shorts, shoes and kit bags, printed on theatre programmes and, above all, published in the ever increasing legions of newspapers and magazines.

THE ADVERTISING AVALANCHE

By the age of 35 the average person will have viewed some 150,000 television commercials, many several times over. This is the equivalent of around 1.5 hours of commercials per week, the same as a full-length feature film.

In the decade from 1981 to 1990 the number of free sheets rose from 550 to over 1,300, while magazines grew 1,367 to 2,373. Media Register – the UK's leading advertising expenditure analysts – pick up about 850,000 display advertisements in newspapers and magazines each year, or around 2,350 per day. Yet they study only 500 of the 9,000 or so publications available. According to the

Register 32,500 branded goods and services are currently being advertised.

Lesson: Your sales message will be fighting for attention against a tidal wave of competing communications. To sell it must break through this barrier.

Our Selective Brain

Our brain can only cope with such massive sensory overload by massive editing and selection. This is carried out by mental mechanisms which act as gate-keepers to higher regions of thought. These censors, operating at a low level in the brain, determine what information will be allowed to get through to the higher regions of thought for consideration. Some signals are ignored entirely, while others are permitted entry below the level of awareness. An example is what has been called the 'cocktail party' phenomenon.

Imagine chatting to a friend at a party in a crowded room and successfully excluding from consideration all the scores of other conversations buzzing around you. However, although ignored at a conscious level, it is likely at least part of that hubbub is being attended to by your brain. If anyone in the room speaks your own name or utters an obscenity (depending on the sort of party it is!) you will instantly switch your attention to whoever uttered those words.

For anybody in selling the degree of sensory overload present in our culture creates a significant barrier to communicating their message. Any sales presentation you make can only contribute to, and must inevitably compete with, this maelstrom of messages.

Furthermore, it will not fall on virgin soil but on the sceptical, cynical, weary and wary advertising-literate mind of twentieth-century consumers.

Under these circumstances persuading prospective customers even to listen and/or look at your sales presentation will be a tough challenge with thousands of alternative messages clamouring for their attention.

The secret of success is to ensure all your sales presentations have built-in MAGIC. This serves as a helpful mnemonic to remind you of the five elements crucial to winning new business.

M = Meaningful to the audience for whom they are intended. The message must be pitched at a level where it is readily understood by your listeners. This depends on a variety of factors, especially their technical knowledge and the type of products/services being sold.

A = Attention grabbing. You have got about sixty seconds to capture their interest and make them see the relevance of your message. If you fail to do so in that first minute, capturing their hearts and minds will become an increasingly futile endeavour.

G = Generate enthusiasm. While this has as much to do with presentational style as content (see Stage Four), it's hard to get enthusiastic about any product or service in which you do not wholeheartedly believe. Your belief is central to sales success. You've got to be red hot to make a prospective customer even warm and that enthusiasm has to be built into the very fabric of your sales presentation in the words you speak, in the illustrations you use and in the demonstrations you make.

I = Involvement. Ever watched one of those plays on stage or television which failed to get you involved? For some reason, perhaps a poor script, bad casting, inadequate acting or ham-fisted directing the drama did nothing to engage you, to make you suspend your disbelief and see the cast as three-dimensional, living beings with real problems and genuine dilemmas. Instead you were unable to see them as other than actors and actresses saying their lines and playing a part.

Good sales presentations have much in common with compelling drama. It is only by involving your audience as completely as possible in the proceedings that you will persuade them to initiate those changes in their thoughts and actions on which new business depends.

As with a theatrical production, such involvement depends on what you have to say, how you say it and the excitement you are able to generate.

C = Content. The last letter in the MAGIC mnemonic brings us back to the first element, that of being meaningful. The elements to which you should draw particular attention depend on who is doing the buying and what is being sold.

ACTION PLAN 10

As I emphasised at the start of this book, every aspect of your business is part of the sales presentation. Every member of your staff, from the most senior executives to the lowliest junior, should be regarded as part of the sales team.

With this in mind, carry out the following six checks on the type of message *your* business is communicating to prospective and existing customers.

1. What message do your telephones communicate?

Call in using an outside line. Fake an accent, give a hard to pronounce name and make a difficult request.

How long did the phone ring before being answered?

Did the voice that came down the line make your company sound friendly and efficient, or curt and disorganised?

How much care did the person answering take when pronouncing your tongue-twisting name?

Was your query dealt with promptly or were you left hanging on the line?

2. What messages do your company premises communicate?

Is your car park free from weeds or litter?

Are there reserved spaces for clients next to the entrance?

Check the lavatories. Are they clean, tidy and free from disagreeable odours? Are soap dispensers full, with plenty of paper towels in the dispenser or a clean roller towel?

3. What message do your fleet vehicles communicate?

What is the condition of your cars, vans, trucks etc., especially those carrying your company name? Dirty, unkept vehicles are bad publicity on wheels, a mobile warning that your firm fails to take pains over details.

How are your company vehicles driven? Do your drivers give consideration to other road users or do they drive selfishly and indifferently?

That 'dithering old fool' your driver carved up at the lights could easily be the chairperson of a company with the potential to become a major customer.

Improve driving by initiating awards for courtesy on the road. Publicise these through the company newsletter and even the local media. By encouraging safer drivers you will reduce maintenance and repair costs, enhance your public image and provide useful publicity.

4. What message does your reception communicate?

How are visitors received in reception? Most of the same rules which apply to telephone callers hold good here too.

5. How courteously does your company manage a customer's time?

Are callers seen promptly? Are they dealt with efficiently and politely? If obliged to wait are they offered explanations and apologies for the delay?

Do service and sales staff on the road keep their appointments?

How long does it take your company to respond to a letter?

You don't know? Find out, fast!

6. What message does your printed material communicate?

The other day my office received a letter from a major company which contained six spelling errors, including that of the managing director's name, and three errors of fact. And this from a consultancy which claimed to specialise in communications!

These six forms of communication may appear trivial and, taken individually, perhaps they are. Yet I have known companies to lose major contracts through their failure to attend to such seemingly minor messages.

KEY POINTS

- Communications are sometimes likened to magic bullets. But they often fail to hit the mark.
- Sources of error include mistakes and ambiguities. But the major barrier to understanding lies in the very personal way we each process information.

- Information overload means your sales message must fight for attention. This can be achieved by providing a positive response to the 'What's in it for me?' question subconsciously, or consciously, posed by every prospect.
- Tailor the content of your presentation to the particular audience for whom it is intended. Use research to tailor that message to their unique needs and levels of expertise.

9 A CHECK LIST BEFORE YOU START

'IT'S VERY IMPORTANT to get your tactics worked out. It's a bit like a General planning a battle. You have to know where everybody's going to be and who's going to do what. Otherwise it will turn into absolute anarchy.'

John Cousins, chairman and creative director, Cousins Advertising

YOU'VE done your research. You've got inside your client's mind and can see your forthcoming sales presentation through their eyes.

You understand the benefits being sold and how to make these appeal to the WIIFM (What's in it for me?) factor.

The time has now come to put it all together: to write your sales presentation script, to create your accompanying visuals, to determine how, where and by whom the presentation should be made, and to prepare yourself and possibly your team, mentally and physically for the challenge of winning new business.

The format and content of your presentation will be largely dependent on the type of audience you are addressing.

A full-blown audio-visual presentation with slides and perhaps a video is clearly inappropriate if you are presenting to one or two people, or where your audience is unused to such overt displays of showmanship.

While making your preparations stay as close as possible to your prospective customers.

Without trespassing too much on their time or patience, get to know them as well as you are able. If possible, identify an ally or 'pitch pal' from whom you can draw useful tips to help your presentation hit the target.

Prior to putting pen to paper, go through one final checklist to ensure you have all the relevant facts at your disposal.

The purpose of such an audit is to confirm your understanding of nine key points regarding the people to whom you will be presenting, plus details of the physical and psychological climate in which that presentation will be made.

1. Who will be there?
2. Who wields the power?
3. Are there any taboos or soft spots?
4. What are they expecting from you?
5. Is the pitch a competitive one?
6. How long have you got?
7. Is it at home or away?
8. What is the layout of the room?
9. Will you have to bring your own audio-visual equipment?

You will find these nine points, together with spaces for your responses, in Action Plan Eleven at the end of this chapter.

Who Will Be There?

How many people will attend your presentation?

What are their names, responsibilities and status within the organisation?

If you're expecting to present to three people and ten turn up, not only will you be short of written documents for them to take away, but it's likely to deal a severe blow to your confidence. One salesman I know arrived at the customer's premises expecting to give an informal talk to two people only to find himself being led into an enormous board room with seating for over twenty. His hopes that this was the only room available in which to meet his two prospects were swiftly dashed when a trolley with twenty-five tea cups was wheeled into the room! Fortunately he was experienced enough to recover from the shock and rapidly restructure his presentation for the far larger audience.

A less confident presenter could well have been so thrown by the changed situation that he, or she, would be lost for words and lose business as a result.

Prevent this from happening to you by checking both well in advance of your appointment and again at the last minute, just to make sure there have been no last-minute changes in plan.

Knowing the names and job titles of your audience helps you focus different aspects of your presentation on the relevant person.

Being aware that the managing director will be sitting in on your presentation, for example, allows you to structure the content in such a way that you devote more time to talking about the company as a whole rather than the individual department which briefed you.

The presence of junior employees should not be overlooked. In many instances it will be them, rather than their bosses, you will be working with. It is therefore critical not to ignore them when making your presentation. Indeed, you should go out of your way to develop a good relationship.

Who Wields the Power?

I have already discussed decision-making units and you should be aware, by this stage, of the general nature of the buying process in that particular company (see Stage Two).

If you have not already done so, make sure you are fully aware of where the buying power lies among your audience.

Pinpointing exactly who makes the decisions to buy is not always a matter of identifying the most senior person present. He or she may be there for 'information only' and, while they may have a say in whether or not you win their business, the final judgement will be delegated to a more junior manager.

Equally it is risky to assume the person who invited you to pitch will be the one who does the hiring. During your research speak to a number of different people within the organisation, to isolate the real power sources. Once you've found out who signs the cheques, make that person the focus of the presentation, addressing your key remarks to them, and asking them for their views and opinions.

Are There Taboos or Soft Spots?

During your pre-presentation planning glean as much background as you can on the politics of the organisation and the people you will be presenting to. The more you discover, the less likely you are to stray into the danger zones that lie hidden in every pitch situation.

Even turning up in the wrong make of car can create a bad impression if the chairperson holds passionate views on supporting a home-based motor industry or dislikes ostentatiousness.

Try to find out about the relationship the company had with their previous supplier – the one you could be replacing. What did they do wrong? What did they do right?

There is no harm in being quite direct with the client by asking them to outline the areas of the previous service which they felt unhappy with. Their response will give you vital clues on how to pitch your proposals. If their main beef was, for example, speed of delivery, you can make sure quick turn-round is central to your presentation.

Remember that even an apparently innocuous comment can act as a red rag to a bull to certain members of your audience.

If part of your presentation includes strong observations, perhaps even criticisms, it's best to try them out on your 'pitch pal' first and, if in doubt, to leave them out.

The same goes for humour. While this can play an important part in your presentation, a joke considered in bad taste will probably kill it dead. For more on the use of jokes and 'amusing' anecdotes, see Chapter 10.

Where possible, find out if any of your audience has been responsible for a particularly successful initiative. You can then drop a few complimentary remarks about it into the presentation: 'I don't know who was behind your recent decision to redesign your retail outlets, but I think it's made a major impact on your high street visibility . . .'

What Are They Expecting From You?

Whether out of excitement at making the presentation or through sheer arrogance, over half of all sales presentations fail simply because their message consists of what the salesperson wants to tell the client, rather than what the client wants to hear.

A classic example in the advertising industry is that of presenting ideas for a TV campaign to a client who clearly cannot afford the budget. No favours will ever be won by taunting clients with the unobtainable.

In many cases you will receive a written brief outlining the requirements for the presentation. Although useful as a guide, this must never be taken as gospel. If it's been written by an individual it may not express the views of colleagues and, if it's been produced by committee, it's likely to contain a number of vague compromises.

Briefing papers should be looked on as consultation documents to be discussed prior to your presentation.

If you get the opportunity, ask for a meeting with your client at their offices to discuss the brief. A reconnaisance trip of this kind will help you get a better feel for the company and a clearer idea of what is expected from you on the day.

Is the Sales Pitch Competitive?

You may be fortunate enough to be the only one invited to make a sales presentation. While this is obviously an advantage it should never be seen as an excuse to become over-confident. If you're up against a number of competitors, your task must be to discover who they are and to identify their weak spots. There's no harm in asking your contact for the names of your opponents, but the normal practice is not to reveal their identity. If they won't tell you, then it's up to you to do your own detective work.

Rumours abound in the advertising industry, for example, that the dustbins of rival agencies are regularly scoured for evidence of work on a pitch.

While I certainly do not suggest descending to such lengths of subterfuge, the odd speculative call to a suspected rival asking to speak to someone working on the 'Acme' business can confirm or dispel your suspicions.

If you discover the names of your competitors, do some homework to identify any weaknesses. It may be that the company is considerably smaller than yours. If this is the case, make sure you extol the virtues of size in your presentation.

How Long Have You Got?

Always ask how much time you have been allocated to make your presentation. Nothing is worse than preparing a ninety-minute sales pitch only to discover your audience has allotted thirty minutes for it.

In a competitive pitch the client will often see a number of presentations on the same day. There is some debate over whether it's better to go first or last. If you are on first the audience is fresh and receptive, but your presentation will be more difficult to recall at the end of the day.

If you are last, your presentation will be fresh in your client's mind when they review what they've heard throughout the day, but they are likely to be suffering from boredom by this stage.

Given a choice of slots, my advice would be to avoid both first and last positions, opting for one somewhere around the middle. However, the so-called 'grave yard' shift, which follows immediately after lunch, is not ideal since your audience is likely to be less alert and more easily bored.

Home or Away?

Making a sales presentation on your own premises is quite different from doing so on the prospect's premises. On your own territory you have a distinct psychological advantage. However, many experienced presenters favour playing away whenever possible.

John Cousins, of Cousins Advertising, says he prefers to pitch at a client's premises because they feel more comfortable on their home ground and he would far rather have the person being sold to feeling comfortable.

Basil Towers, chairman and managing director of Christow Consultants, agrees it's better to make the presentation on your clients' territory: 'They can actually see you fitting in – or not, as the case may be.'

Given that a sales presentation is a process of actively initiating a change, and that – as I have already explained – all change arouses a certain amount of uncertainty and apprehension, this would seem a sensible course of action.

When making a presentation in your own premises check the following points.

1. Can it comfortably hold all the people you expect to attend? You need sufficient capacity to take a few unexpected visitors and still not feel too cramped.
2. Can you control the temperature and air quality in this room? Feeling too hot or too cold creates significant barriers to sales success since your audience will feel stressed and more irritable. The same applies to an overly stuffy room. If you intend to close the windows, to reduce street noise and maybe draw the curtains in order to project slides etc., bear in mind that even a few people rapidly raise the temperature of a medium-sized room.
3. Can your visitors find your premises easily? It is a good idea to fax clear instructions, including any landmarks.
4. When they arrive can they park easily? If you do not have your own parking facilities, the map should include details of the nearest car park.
5. Are the receptionists expecting them, do they know their names and why they will be attending? A simple, low-cost and courteous touch is to have a welcome board in reception and print up the names of visitors. But if you do this be very careful to ensure that all names are all spelled correctly and that any titles – Dr etc. – are included.
6. If you intend serving tea, coffee or some other beverage organise this in advance. Try and find out whether any of your visitors prefer decaffinated coffee or herbal tea.

And always serve freshly brewed beverages in real china – clean, attractive and definitely unchipped!

What is the Room Layout?

When presenting in somebody else's territory always ask about the room where the presentation is to be held and, where possible, inspect it beforehand. Some advertising agencies send someone round with a Polaroid to take pictures of the meeting room so that detailed plans about who will stand where can be made.

There can be nasty surprises in store for anyone who expects to deliver their beautifully crafted pitch in a room that befits the occasion. It is not unusual to find yourself cramped into a corner of someone's office, or in a room with no table or nowhere to sit.

The size of the room and its ability to be darkened are critical factors when preparing the visual aids for the pitch. It's no good turning up with your slide carousel only to discover there are no curtains or blinds in the room.

Check the location and types of power points. If you intend using visual aids, can the cables be connected to power sources easily and safely? Cables trailing across the floor pose a real risk in a darkened room and breaking your client's leg is probably not the best way to make your presentation memorable!

The type of socket should also be checked to ensure that it will support the power demands of your equipment. Some years ago I was lecturing to IBM managers at Jesus College, Cambridge. It wasn't until we arrived that it was discovered the hall of residence, where my presentation was to take place, was fitted entirely with 5 amp instead of the expected 13 amp sockets. This had been done by the college authorities to prevent students boiling kettles and cooking in their rooms.

As a result not only did none of the plugs fit, but having managed to connect up the equipment, switching on the computers and printers required for my presentation overloaded the system, blew the circuit breakers and plunged us all into darkness.

Will You Need to Bring Your Own Audio-Visual Equipment?

Once again, do not assume your clients will have their own overhead or slide projector, or that they will remember to lay one on for your presentation even when asked to do so.

If bringing your own slides, check the slide trays will fit into their projector. Most well-equipped companies use the Kodak carousel types, with circular trays. But this is not always the case. Having to change all the trays immediately prior to your presentation is not only time-consuming but stressful and communicates a lack of efficiency on your part.

Occasionally you may be asked to make a sales presentation before a very large audience at a conference or seminar. If so, check with the production team whether slide projection is from the front or rear. In some instances projectors are concealed from the audience behind the screen.

This means the slides have to be reversed, as against front projection, to appear the right way around to your audience. A colleague of mine on a sales tour of Australia made the mistake of not checking out every venue and arrived 10 minutes before making a presentation to 500 managers to discover the hall used rear projection. Since he was showing more than 200 slides, this proved to be a considerable problem.

Under such circumstances it is also probable that you will use some form of sound amplification system. This could consist of a stand microphone, a hand-held mike which may work either via a lead or by radio, or a professional radio microphone which clips to your jacket or tie.

Stand microphones, especially when these are attached to the podium, are truly horrible things for any presenter not already tied to the podium or table by a script, whether read from paper or off an autocue device. Since reading a sales presentation, as I shall explain in the next stage, is extremely bad practice and to be avoided at almost any cost, there will be no reason – microphone apart – to stand behind the podium or a table. By doing so you restrict your movement and block off most of your body, so denying the audience important body language signals.

Radio microphones are by far the best if, like me, you want to be able to move around during your presentation.

Hand-held radio mikes are less suitable for two reasons. First, it takes practice to hold the microphone in exactly the right position to get consistent sound quality. Move it even slightly away from your mouth and you will go 'off-mike', making it far harder for your audience to hear the message.

The second problem is that your ability to illustrate points using gestures is severely limited. A compromise is the trailing or Lavaliere microphone which, although attached to a long lead, clips on to your jacket or tie. The only danger here is the risk of tripping over your own lead. Radio microphones do, however, have one potential drawback. They will detect any transmissions on their wavelength. Normally this shouldn't be a problem, but it can happen. Once, while making a presentation in a London hotel, I was horrified to discover my microphone was picking up a local minicab company! Fortunately this came to light during the rehearsal, but if it had happened in the middle of a sales pitch the results would have been embarrassing to say the least.

One final point about radio mikes is always to have a fall-back position in case of failure. It should not happen but it can and does. Always have a second microphone, even if it is only the one on the lectern, for use in an emergency.

Finally consider how you will change your slides or overheads. A remote-control slide projector which can be operated from the lectern, using an infra-red or radio remote, is the best option.

With overheads you should, ideally, use an assistant to avoid having to make a major part of your presentation with your back to the audience. If you do ask somebody to change your OHPs, rehearse the actions so that changes proceed smoothly and without too much prompting.

The day before the pitch, put in a call to confirm your attendance and to remind them of any equipment you need. If bringing your own equipment be sure to remember:

1. spare bulb for projectors;
2. extension lead;
3. spare fuse;
4. screwdriver.

By completing this check list you increase confidence, reduce anxiety and make it less likely that something will go wrong before you even start.

ACTION PLAN 11

In advance of your sales presentation complete the following check list. You will find it helpful to photocopy the details so that they can be used for each new pitch.

CLIENT:

DATE OF SALES PRESENTATION:

CONTACT PHONE NUMBERS:

1. WHO WILL BE THERE?

a) ....

b) ....

c) ....

d) ....

e) ....

f) ....

2. WHO WIELDS THE POWER?

a) ....

b) ....

c) ....

d) ....

e) ....

f) ....

3. ARE THERE ANY TABOOS OR SOFT SPOTS?

....

....

4. WHAT ARE THEY EXPECTING FROM YOU?

....

....

5. IS THE PITCH A COMPETITIVE ONE? YES/NO (Circle as appropriate) If YES:
Who are my competitors?

COMPANY A
STRENGTHS

....

....

....

WEAKNESSES

. . . .

. . . .

. . . .

COMPANY B
STRENGTHS

. . . .

. . . .

. . . .

WEAKNESSES

. . . .

. . . .

. . . .

COMPANY C

STRENGTHS

. . . .

. . . .

. . . .

WEAKNESSES

. . . .

. . . .

. . . .

6. HOW LONG HAVE I GOT?

. . . .

7. HOME OR AWAY?

HOME/AWAY (Circle as appropriate)

IF AWAY:

8. WHAT IS THE LAYOUT OF THE ROOM?

Sketch out the details below. Indicate positions of power points and windows. Check that windows can be blacked out if you intend to use visual aids. Make sure you and the screen can be seen easily by all members of your audience.

9. WILL I HAVE TO BRING MY OWN AUDIO-VISUAL EQUIPMENT?

YES/NO (Circle as appropriate)

If YES, equipment to be taken includes (Tick as appropriate)

a) Overhead projector ☐
b) Slide projector ☐
c) Video/TV ☐
d) Computer ☐
e) Other ....

If equipment is to be provided by the client, check that it is available on the day immediately before your presentation.

CHECK MADE:

KEY POINTS

- Fortune favours the well prepared. Go through a nine-point check list before starting to prepare your presentation.
- Although there is some debate about whether it is better to present to clients in your premises or their's, playing away is probably the better option since it makes the clients feel more comfortable.
- When presenting away from your own premises always try and visit the location in advance to check layout and details of power points, blinds on windows etc.

10 PUTTING IT ALL TOGETHER . .

> 'THE DISCIPLINE of writing something down is the first step towards making it happen. There is something about putting your thoughts on paper that forces you to get down to specifics. That way, it is hard to deceive yourself, or anybody else.'
>
> *Lee Iacocca*

WE HAVE already seen how aspects of your prospective customer's personality can influence the type of presentation he or she is most likely to find involving and persuasive (see pages 117–120). The nature of the product or service you have to sell will also significantly influence the expectations of your audience.

Before starting to write down your sales presentation consider which information should be included and how those key selling points should be ordered, explained and illustrated. Here are some general guidelines as to the type of information different types of buyers expect and need before deciding to buy.

You sell: High priced and infrequently purchased products, such as capital equipment, specialised instruments or products demanding a high level of technical knowledge and expertise on the part of a purchaser.
Your likely audience will be: Engineers, technical staff, management, purchasing executives.
They will expect: Technical detail with facts and figures illustrated by graphs and tables.

You sell: Supplies, replacement equipment and components.
Your likely audience will be: Engineers, office managers, technical staff, management.
They will expect: Information about its special features and a clear explanation of the differences between models. Use illustrations to provide visual assurance that what you are selling precisely matches their needs.

You sell: Metals, chemicals, plastics, solvents, lubricants and similar materials.
Your likely audience will be: Engineers, technical staff, management.
They will expect: A clear and authoritative description of the physical, chemical and performance properties of the material, together with its specifications. Detailed performance and application data should be provided and illustrated. They will be seeking reassurance on quality control, capacity and general reliability.

You sell: Specialised consultancy and other technical services.
Your likely audience will be: Relevant managers plus possibly technical staff.
They will expect: A description of your experience in this field. Include information about your company's size and

track record, together with a list of previous clients. They will be seeking reassurance on your company's ability to deliver on promises of quality, performance and dependability.

The above suggestions also apply when preparing copy for trade catalogues and supporting material either sent in advance of your sales presentation or provided at the time.

The Structure Of A Sales Presentation

All presentations can be rated on two dimensions, how light or serious they are and the degree of formality involved.

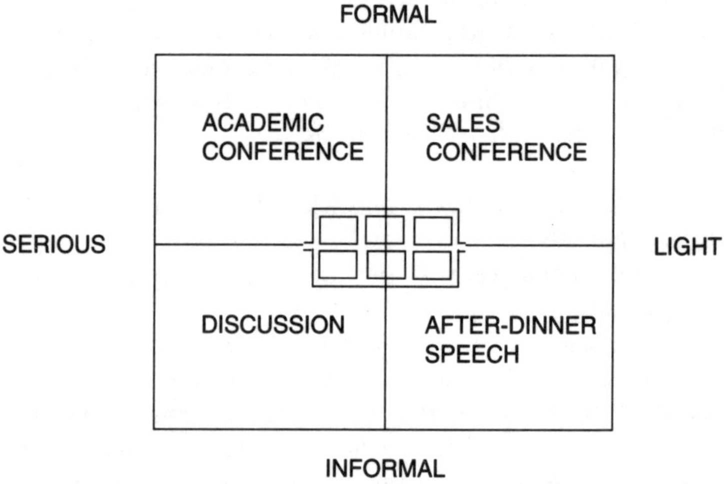

FORMAL

SERIOUS			LIGHT
	ACADEMIC CONFERENCE	SALES CONFERENCE	
	DISCUSSION	AFTER-DINNER SPEECH	

INFORMAL

As the illustration shows, academic papers given at scientific conferences tend to be both formal and serious.

Scripts are usually read – frequently badly – by the speaker, who stands rigidly behind a lectern.

In complete contrast an after-dinner speech, intended to entertain rather than to inform, is light and informal. Experienced after-dinner speakers talk either entirely 'off the cuff' or using the briefest notes to remind them of key points.

A sales conference tends to be reasonably formal although efforts are usually made, perhaps by introducting celebrity guest speakers, to entertain as well as inform.

Finally, discussions with colleagues which take place during working hours are generally fairly serious but informal.

The effective sales presentation is positioned in the central zone of this matrix, indicated by the box illustration opposite.

It should be sufficiently formal for the content to be taken seriously. You are certainly not expected to treat the matter casually or flippantly. But while many presentations are also fairly serious, they are also expected to catch the imagination and hold the attention.

Clearly, the levels of formality/informality and light/serious content will vary according to the type of audience you are addressing and the nature of the product being sold. But veering too far in either direction on these variables is a mistake.

In order to achieve this delicate balance, script and visual aids must be exactly suited to your sales purpose. So too must your method of delivery. The persuasive power of even the best script and most attention-grabbing visual aids will be significantly diminished if sloppily or amateurishly presented.

Beating the Boredom Barrier

Some sales presentations are so uninspiring and ineffective they offer a positive disincentive to buy. Avoid creating boredom barriers to winning new business by keeping two points in mind.

1. Make sure your presentation is concise and carefully targeted. Confine the contents to the things your audience really needs to know. Provide sufficient

information to support your key sales points without overwhelming the audience. Check carefully for any irrelevant information, anything your listeners either already know or do not need to know. If in doubt put yourself in the prospective customer's position by asking: 'If I had to make that buying decision, what would I want to be told?'

2. Deliver your presentation in a relaxed and chatty manner. Tension and anxiety are contagious and will make your listeners uneasy, even if they are not always sure why they feel such discomfort. Given that, as I explained in Chapter 7, selling arouses a certain amount of apprehension, by seeking actively to initiate a change in the buyer's mind-set and behaviour, the last thing you want to do is add to such unease. The more relaxed you are, the more relaxed and receptive will be your audience. Practical procedures for controlling these all too common nerves will be described in Part Four.

   Unless these two components of the sales presentation – content and delivery – are managed correctly your audience is likely to remember no more than 5 per cent of what you have told them.

Putting Your Words to the KISS Test

After writing your presentation script apply the KISS test by asking: 'Have I *k*ept *i*t *s*imple and *s*traightforward?' Here are twelve ways to ensure that not a word or line fails this important test.

1. Start by writing down your key points as briefly as possible. Now develop these using as few words as possible. Have a clear goal in mind and work steadily towards its accomplishment.

Follow the advice of Socrates who, when asked by a stranger how he could get to Mount Olympus, replied simply: 'Just make certain every step you take is headed in that direction.'

Avoid the temptation of going off at a tangent, repeating yourself, or including facts and figures simply to impress. Start rambling on and your audience will rapidly switch off.

Keep your sentences short, since overly wordy ones increase the risk of your listeners forgetting what was said at the start by the time you arrive at the finish!

2. Make certain your presentation fits the available time without forcing you to rush through the final points.

While this is especially important when a pitch is competitive, with several firms presenting to the same group on the same day, no audience will thank you or feel impressed if you go beyond your allotted time.

Bear in mind the fact that a presentation always takes longer to perform in practice than in rehearsal, usually by about 25 per cent. A presentation taking twelve minutes at rehearsal will require fifteen minutes on the day.

Develop the discipline of thinking about your product or service in a focused manner.

One useful exercise is to summarise your main benefits in no more than fifty words. This is the number of words which can be read in twenty seconds at a reasonable and easily understood rate of delivery. As a guide there are exactly fifty words in this fairly short paragraph.

3. Write for speaking not for reading. Spoken and written words differ significantly with sentences which read smoothly sounding false and stilted when spoken aloud.

Prevent your presentation from sounding 'ink stained' by reading it aloud into a tape recorder and then replaying the script. Write for your own particular spoken style, using sentence structures and words which flow easily from your lips. Never try saying anything which feels uncomfortable.

Edit and re-edit until the words sound natural when spoken. This does not mean that you should revise your presentation to death. After replacing any words, speak the whole passage aloud to ensure that the rhythm has been preserved.

You will achieve a relaxed conversational style more easily if you imagine yourself talking to a friend instead of writing for an audience of strangers.

You may also find it easier to dictate than write down your presentations. If you are not used to dictating it may be difficult, at first, to marshal your thoughts. However, with a little practice the technique becomes quite easy.

4. When you start drafting your presentation do not worry too much about getting the content 100 per cent correct. It is far better to allow your thoughts to flow, even at the expense of some sloppy sentences or poorly constructed paragraphs.

Never mind that the copy seems disjointed in the first draft. Professional writers and presenters know that it is always far easier to edit down material than to get it down in the first instance. Strive for total perfection and you'll never get the pitch written at all.

5. Maintaining a fast writing pace keeps your creative juices flowing and helps ensure that the words will sound natural when you speak them aloud.

Once your ideas are flowing never stop to reread what you have written or you may dry up again.

If you don't know where to begin, just write down any thoughts related to your presentation which come to mind.

Still stuck? Then, instead of trying to write down those thoughts, just speak them out loud. Putting ideas into words often breaks down any blocks to creativity.

6. Use the words 'You' and 'Yours' at the start of the presentation so that each member of the audiences can easily see what is 'in it for them'.

7. Capture and retain your audience's attention by painting word pictures for them, which emphasise the benefits you are offering.

But never use the word 'benefit' which sounds too much like a piece of sales jargon. Instead, describe the results which purchasing your service or product will afford.

When starting to write, list these benefits using just a few key words, the fewer the better. Now create a mini-speech around those key words. Remember to use the feature to benefit conversion phrase 'which means that ...'.

8. While you should employ any relevant technical expressions and terms when speaking to a specialist audience, avoid all suggestions of jargon. Words whose only purpose is to demonstrate how smart you are compared to your audience will only confuse, irritate and alienate them.

For the same reason ruthlessly cut out any words which sound pompous, ponderous, patronising or pedantic.

9. Research shows that our memory is best for information which we hear first and last. It's the bits which come in the middle that cause the greatest problems of recall.

Psychologists call this the 'primacy' and 'recency' effects. Professionals advise: 'Tell them what you are going to tell them, tell them, tell them what you have told them.'

Structure your sales presentation so that it:

- starts by outlining the key reasons your audience should be buying your product or service;
- develops these themes in a concise and relevant way;
- repeats the key benefits.

10. Avoid anything which seems to attack your audience's belief or values, whether these are corporate, cultural or religious. This is especially important when pitching to clients from a culture different from your own.

Make certain that nothing in your presentation will antagonise or appear to patronise your audience.

11. Use positive, energising words when writing your

presentation and make certain they all work hard. In a short pitch you cannot afford to carry passengers.

Banish phrases which add nothing to your message, eg:

'It goes without saying ...' – then why say it?

'It's hardly necessary to repeat ...' – so why repeat it?

'I would like to start by saying ...' – just say it!

'A lot of time and effort has gone into this presentation ...' – your audience is not the slightest bit interested in how much time or effort was involved, they are only interested in the outcome.

'I feel sure you will understand ...' – don't put money on it!

Also to be avoided are 'filler' remarks such as 'Which reminds me of a story ...' and 'In conclusion ...'. These make the presentation sound stilted and formal.

12. Choose words and phrases which communicate confidence, purpose and action. High energy words which excite and stimulate people include:

appreciate	assurance	confidence
convenience	courtesy	discover
dependable	easy	economy
efficient	enjoyment	expert
experienced	fun	genuine
growth	guarantee	health
help	love	modern
money	necessary	new
original	peace of mind	popular
pride	profitable	protection
prestige	quality	reputation
results	save	security
service	share	stimulating

stylish
understand
your
successful
unexcelled
thank you
you

Some of these words reflect deep feelings, while others offer realistic and believable solutions to problems, assurances of safety, security, fun and happiness.

But beware of words and phrases which, although they possess plenty of energy, come across as insincere or mere sales hype. These include:

between you and me
do you follow me?
how are you?
really
you ought
you must!
brand new
fabulous
out of this world
unbelievable
you should

Using Humour

A well-timed and relevant comment, anecdote, or even a joke can help your audience feel more relaxed, increase their positive feelings towards you and improve recall of key points. But beware.

Irrelevant, off-target or mistimed stories will have exactly the opposite effect, making your audience tense, embarrassed and disinclined to pay further attention.

Here are some points to watch out for.

- Unless you are extremely skilled at telling jokes – and that should be the opinion of disinterested third parties rather than you or your immediate family – don't even attempt them.

  Timing is critical to getting a laugh with the majority of jokes and timing, as any professional funny man or women will tell you, takes a great deal of practice and no little natural talent to perfect.

- Anecdotes and amusing observations are another matter entirely. If your research has revealed an 'in-joke', topical reference or insider jibe, then by all means use it. Such remarks aid you in that all-important task of being seen as a 'team player' or somebody who thinks like the rest of those present and is already on the inside track.
- Only use humour which is upbeat and spirited, never depressing or discouraging.
- Only tell stories which include your whole audience, rather than invite some people to laugh at others.
- Only tell stories *you* find funny. If the joke or anecdote fails to amuse the teller, it's hardly likely to set the audience rocking with laughter.
- Never use humour you are uncomfortable with. Tell a story which makes you even slightly embarrassed and your audience will feel even more so.
- Match the humour to the tastes and background of your audience but never risk giving offence. A single offensive story could be sufficient to cost you an otherwise certain sale. For this reason I advise you never to tell rude, risqué, vulgar or obscene jokes. Avoid racial and religious jokes like the plague.
- If one of your stories dies, don't let that throw you. Just press on with the presentation. Never, ever try to recover the lost joke by making a comment such as 'That was supposed to be funny . . .' or 'Well, I find that amusing . . .'. Just pretend it was never meant to amuse and get on with the business of selling.

WORD POWER AT WORK

A New York advertising copy writer recalls the time he was down on his luck after being made redundant. Walking past Central Park one sunny May morning he came across a beggar holding a placard which read: 'I am blind'. Few of the hurrying New Yorkers bothered even to glance at the man, let alone pause to drop a coin in his box.

Moved by the beggar's plight the copy writer badly wanted to help.

He explained he had no spare cash but would like to use his skill with words to change the beggar's message by adding four more words. When he passed by a few hours later the man's collecting box was full and people were eager to give him a hand-out. Those four words which had proved so powerfully persuasive?

The message now read: 'I am blind. And it is spring!'

Lesson: It's not how many words you use which matters, but how you choose them and use them.

Checking Your Script One Last Time

After completing your script, perform these six final checks: only tick the point when completely satisfied your answer is YES. If in doubt rewrite, then check again. Ask the following.

1. Does my presentation build the case for buying? Do the facts I introduce support one another to create a solid and logical structure? [YES/NO]
2. Is my script prepared in such a way as to ensure a smooth, comfortable delivery? [YES/NO]
3. Are all abstract thoughts and proposals supported by sound evidence, accurate figures and firm facts? [YES/NO]
4. Will my audience understand all the words being used, including technical expressions? [YES/NO]
5. Is every word used correctly and precisely? [YES/NO]

6. Does my presentation build to a clear conclusion that my audience will understand and remember? [YES/NO]

Why the Eyes Have It

A picture, they say, is worth a thousand words. And this is supported by research which suggests that information we take in through our eyes is a thousand times more effective than that which we gain via our ears.

When it comes to sales presentations, a picture – or better still several pictures – can certainly make your sales challenge a thousand times easier.

Studies confirm that when visual aids are used there is a significant increase in retention:

Presentation	After 3 hours	After 3 days
Tell only	70%	10%
Show only	72%	20%
Show and tell	85%	65%

Other benefits identified by research include these:

- group consensus becomes 21 per cent more likely;
- the time required to make a presentation can be cut by up to 40 per cent.

Visuals enable you to:

- communicate ideas faster than using the spoken word alone;
- arouse and hold the interest of your audience;
- explain complex ideas more easily and accurately;
- appear more organised and professional;
- reinforce and enhance your spoken words, and increase the probability that *all* your sales message will be understood;

- add variety to an otherwise dry or serious presentation;
- take some of the pressure off you by diverting your audience's attention;
- cut across language barriers (important for an international or multicultural audience);
- help clarify different opinions and viewpoints in a controversial subject area.

General Points on Visuals

When using any type of visual aids bear in mind the following points.

- Focus on only one idea per visual.
- Choose the text carefully. The fewer words the better.
- Avoid creating cluttered visuals. Concise bullet points are easier to read than long sentences.
- Underline the title.
- Separate and number each point.
- Make certain that every visual you use has a clear message. Never be tempted to display pictures, charts or tables unless they are *essential* to the point being made. If a visual adds nothing to the presentation then leave it out.
- Explain each visual as it is projected.
- Always maintain eye-contact with your audience, never turn away to address your comments to the flipchart or screen since this means turning your back on the audience.
- When presenting to a large group read each visual aloud to ensure that even those at the back understand it.
- Never begin or end your sales presentation with a visual. You and not your visuals are what people came to see.

Types of Visual Aids

There are seven main types of visual aid:

1. handouts
2. flip charts

3. overhead projectors
4. slide projectors
5. video and CD-ROM
6. computer-generated images
7. film projector.

Your choice will depend on a number of factors, including availability of equipment, cost, location, transportation and the type of audience to whom you are making your presentation.

1. Handouts

For: Quick and fairly easy to produce, handouts provide a reminder of the key points of your presentation which your audience can take away.

Preparing handouts

There will be occasions when a client wants to see the presentation documents several days before the pitch in order to give a more considered response to what you are saying. Unless specifically asked to do so, however, it is better to give your handouts to the audience at the end rather than the start of a presentation. If they have the material beside them people flick around with it, which is distracting and prevents you receiving their full attention.

Some handouts are capable of being read and followed by someone who wasn't at the presentation. This degree of preparation is worth while when you know some of the influential decision makers will be unable to attend your presentation. Most of the time bullet points serving as memory joggers are sufficient. Many buying decisions are based on the presentation itself with handouts never even being read. When preparing handouts keep these points in mind:

- They must look polished and professional. Check lay-out, spelling and grammar carefully. Always ask a third party to read your copy since it is very hard for you as author to

spot your own mistakes. We tend to see what we expect to see instead of what is actually there. Do nouns and verbs agree? Are pronouns used properly?
- If graphics are used make them simple and straightforward.

2. Flip charts

For: Flexible, versatile and easy to use, flip charts should only be used with audiences of fewer than forty.

They can be persuasive if presenting to graduate buyers, especially engineers or scientists, since their very simplicity and informality evokes memories of a university tutorial rather than a slick sales presentation.

Against: Your presentation will appear amateurish to sophisticated corporate buyers used to a more 'bells and whistles' type of presentation.

Sometimes the sheets bleed through, spoiling the paper beneath. Easels fall over when bumped and marker pens rapidly dry out if left uncapped.

Preparing flip charts

- Follow the 5 × 5 rule for each chart. No more than five lines with no more than five words in each line.
- Use green marker pens in low light because this colour has maximum luminosity under dim conditions.
- Avoid blue – it reduces attention.
- Red is best for attracting attention and creating greatest recall. It should be used to provide bullet points identifying key benefits and underlining factors or figures you are especially eager to impress on your audience's memory. But never use it with points you are less eager to emphasise.
- When building to a sales point start using cooler colours, such as green, and then proceeding to warmer ones, like yellow, orange and red.
- Prepare most of your pages in advance so as not to waste

time having to write out a whole sheet while talking. Leave gaps for the key facts and figures to be completed during the presentation.

- Underline key words and phrases or place them in boxes.
- Use pictures to enliven the presentation. If you are not much of an artist these can be traced on to the sheets.
- Bring extra markers with you in all the colours you will need.

Writing on charts

- Tape the legs of the easel to the floor to prevent it being knocked over.
- Set the pad low enough to flip the sheets over easily if this is how you intend changing them.
- If you intend tearing sheets off the pad, practise this technique as follows. Place your hands on the top corner of the sheet and start to tear. Using the hand closest to the easel, rip the sheet carefully along its perforation, lifting it upwards slightly as you do so. This prevents unsightly, ragged edges and torn sheets.
- When using a lapel or Lavaliere microphone, keep the sheets clear of it to avoid unnecessary noise.
- Write the key points of your presentation on the edges of the pages as a memory aid. By speeding your delivery this will help retain your audience's attention.

3. Overhead projectors (OHPs)

For: OHPs are best when presenting to audiences of between ten and fifty people. If addressing fewer than ten, either handouts or a flip chart are usually easier and simpler.

Most medium-sized and all large companies will have at least one of these display units, which is just as well because even 'portable' models are fairly awkward to carry around.

Transparencies can be prepared quickly and fairly easily either by hand or using a computer-driven printer to produce more sophisticated visuals.

OHPs can be used in rooms with a higher level of illumination than slide projectors.

Against: They are fairly unsophisticated and smack more of a technical training session than a sales presentation. However, for reasons given above this less 'professional' feel may lend credibility to pitches aimed at technical and specialist audiences.

A more important consideration is the noise from the projector's high-powered cooling fan and the glare of light on the screen.

Unless you are constantly moving to and fro between the OHP and your speaking position in front of your audience, you will need a well-rehearsed assistant to change transparencies for you.

Producing the transparencies

- When not on the OHP the transparency should be easy to read at a distance of 6 ft. This will ensure the image can be seen easily on projection.
- If possible avoid using handwritten OHP transparencies as it looks amateurish. When you do have to write make sure your handwriting is neat. Large, thick script conveys an impression of confidence, while small, thin letters create the impression of weakness. If you are planning to jot down points while the audience looks on, pre-write them on the border then copy them out.
- Use a maximum of six lines with no more than six words per line.
- Use capitals and lower case letters rather than all upper case since this is easier to read.
- Never write words vertically – they are difficult to read.
- Use dark colours such as red, black, blue or green rather than orange, yellow or light brown. Keep the chosen colours consistent with your pitch. If, for example, you decide to write headings in blue and the main text in black, continue doing so throughout.

- Use different colours and type styles to highlight contrasting ideas.
- Position the key sales points high up on the transparency for emphasis.
- Two or even three transparencies can be used as overlays to build a sales point, making each in a new colour. But never attempt complicated overlays unless you have plenty of time to practise.
- Write key points from your presentation on the card mounts to jog your memory. That way no one will notice you referring to them. Position these bullet points so they can be read while you are facing the audience.

Projection techniques

- Keep your projector turned off until you are ready to reveal the next transparency. Alternatively, use a large sheet of card or paper to cover the whole screen until you are ready to show that transparency. Using normal weight paper you can block off parts of the image while still reading the next points on your transparency with the projector switched on.
- Practise uncovering the transparency on cue with the content of your speech.
- Never remove a transparency while the OHP is turned on. The glare is painful and it looks unprofessional.
- Avoid odd-shaped images by adjusting the tilt of the screen. If the top of the image is wider than the base, tilt the top of the screen towards the projector. If the bottom of the image is too wide, move the top of the screen away from the projector.
- Be sure the table on which your OHP stands is solid and stable. Even a small judder on the support becomes a distracting movement on the screen.
- Use a pointer to identify key points on the screen rather than doing so directly on the transparency. This allows

you to remain facing the audience rather than standing with your back to them.

- Avoid walking through the projector beam – it's amateurish and distracting.
- Always have a back-up OHP or one with two bulbs.

4. Slide projectors

For: Probably the most widely used of all the visual aids. The equipment is sufficiently sophisticated to provide high quality results at a reasonable budget and they can be used with very large groups.

Slide projection is the form of audio-visual (AV) with which corporate buyers will be most familiar. They help to ensure that your presentation looks carefully prepared.

Projectors can be operated by infra-red or radio remote control at a distance, allowing you to remain at the front of the room and still control all the functions – including focus on many of the higher priced projectors.

Against: The room must be suitably darkened to ensure a clear image, although there should always be enough light for the audience to take notes and to see you clearly.

Slide projectors are less likely to be standard items, except in large companies, which means you will have to bring your own.

Slides require longer-term preparation so last-minute changes cannot be accommodated.

Unlike OHP transparencies or flip charts it is far harder to change the running order of the slides once your presentation has begun. This commits you to a particular sequence of information, preventing you from responding to any changes of direction dictated by the audience.

Producing your slides

Computer-generated 35 mm slides can be made in-house – if you have several thousand pounds to invest in the necessary technology – but are normally made to your specifications by a specialist house.

Alternatively, you can create the presentation using an in-house computer and then send the finished slides, as computer data on a disc, to a specialist house which will create the actual photographic slides.

- If designing your own slides, be careful not to make them too fancy. Excessive embellishment reduces understanding, especially on charts or graphs.
- When discussing figures support your comments with a visual. Use bar or pie graphs to illustrate relative values, for instance if comparing unit sales of trucks by four different manufacturers.
- Bar charts are better than pie charts for presenting statistical information because they are easier to interpret.
- Place the bars in a bar graph in either ascending or descending order, since this pattern is both easier to see and visualise.
- Never use longer bars to illustrate a lesser quantity of anything. For example, if comparing cities by the amount of crime experienced, using a longer bar for the one with the least crime would give a completely misleading effect. People associate longer bars with a greater, not a lesser, amount.
- No more than four pieces of information should be presented on a single slide since people are incapable of keeping more than this number in their minds at any one time.
- Write headlines in both capital and lower case letters rather than capitals only.
- If using an illustration write the words below the picture. Because our eyes tend to look at illustrations first any words written above the picture create a visual conflict. When the words are under the image, however, the viewer's gaze need no longer battle against gravity, but can travel naturally and comfortably downwards.

Tips for fault-free slide presentations

- Practise using the remote control. If using a cord remote check that it is long enough to allow you to go where you want.
- Mark the forward button clearly – a piece of white tape will do – so that you do not make the mistake of suddenly reversing the slides.
- Start and finish the presentation with full house lights since eye-contact is essential at these times (see Stage Four). Have house lights raised when you want the audience to focus on you, while describing a central benefit for example.
- Stand to the right of the screen as seen by the audience. This is better because your audience will be reading slide text from left to right. If you are standing on the right, their eyes will follow the lines back to you. Stand on the left and their gaze must constantly be drawn back to look at yours. This can create subconscious antagonism and sales resistance.

5. Video and CD-ROM drives

Still or moving images, illustrations and graphics, can be put on video, and still pictures only transferred to compact discs to produce a sophisticated presentation using a new system developed by Kodak. Image CD-ROMS can be shown on a TV screen, using a special player, or via a computer fitted with CD-ROM drive.

For: They produce a slick and sophisticated presentation capable of providing audiences with a great deal of information in an attention-grabbing way.

Both videos and CD-ROM drives can be operated from a distance using infra-red remote controls. The CD-ROM drives developed by Kodak also offer facilities for automatically changing the images at a pre-set rate and in any order you wish. Sections of the image can be enlarged and the whole picture rotated through 360 degrees.

Provided you have sufficient monitors, or use a projection television, this method of presentation is suitable for showing to medium-sized audiences in rooms with a fairly high level of ambient light. Where money is no object and you have a long time to prepare, it is even possible to install a video-wall.

This impressive battery of monitors creates, as the name suggests, something like a sheer wall of images.

These highly complex and costly devices are generally confined to major sales presentations, for instance the launching of a new car.

Against: The system lacks flexibility and requires expensive equipment both to show and prepare the visual aid material. The cost of preparing such aids is also high and time-consuming.

Transferring images to CD-ROM is a specialist and time-consuming task which cannot, at present, be carried out in-house.

Being complex equipment there is greater risk of it breaking down at the least appropriate moments.

If unable to fix it yourself take along a technician who can. Double check everything before the presentation starts and then keep your fingers firmly crossed!

Tips for fault-free video presentations

- Cue your video tape carefully before the presentation begins. Never advance or rewind the tape while your audience looks on.
- Brief segments of video tape are better than lengthy clips since they take attention away from you, the really important presenter, for too long.
- When bringing video equipment in from the car on a cold or damp night, allow time for it to warm up so as to prevent condensation causing the tape to adhere to the heads.
- When running video from another country be aware that

different standards are non-compatible. For example, tapes recorded in the US using their NTSC system will not play on UK and European PAL machines.

- Check from all parts of the auditorium to ensure your TV screen is large enough to be seen comfortably by every member of your audience. If there are problems install additional monitors.

6. Computer-generated images

Lap-top computers are now capable of generating excellent colour images which can be shown on a standard computer monitor or else projected using an overhead projector on which a special computer screen is placed.

For: Sophisticated presentation. Slides can be updated or changed at short notice.

Against: Without additional monitors or a projection system they are only suitable for use with small groups.

Image quality is less good than with photographic slides, leading to loss of definition.

The equipment is expensive – although if you already have a lap-top or easily transportable computer you are half-way there.

Tip: If buying a lap-top computer with the intention of using it for presentations the most important factor is not battery life, disk drive, memory or processor speed, but the ability to generate 256-colour images in standard VGA resolution.

The difference between 16-colour and 256-colour graphs, including scanned images, shaded backgrounds and animation, is remarkable.

7. Film projectors

These are generally out of favour, despite the fact that there is evidence to show some audiences take a filmed sequence more seriously than the same images shown on video. However, this increased credibility is more than outweighed by the cost of producing filmed material and the awkwardness of projecting it.

ACTION PLAN 12

Practise the points described in this chapter either by analysing an existing sales presentation, perhaps one you made in the recent past, or by creating one.

Remember that every word must work for you. There is no room for redundancy.

Check that your presentation does the following.

- Describes benefits not just features.
- Has relevance to the audience. Use your research to determine this crucial fact. Is it pitched at the right level of technical sophistication? Does it meet their needs?
- Have you included the necessary reassurances to reduce the threat posed by change?

Finally, get a colleague to role-play your prospect. He, or she, should have read all the research background so as to be able to think like that customer. Take notice of their feedback and make any adjustments necessary.

KEY POINTS

- Match your content to the needs and expectations of your intended audience. Put yourself in their position and ask what *you* would want to know in order to make an informed buying decision.
- Keep your presentation concise and carefully targeted.

- Deliver it in a relaxed manner using the techniques described in Stage Four.
- Check that every phrase and sentence passes the KISS test. Ask yourself: 'Am I keeping it simple and straightforward'?
- Make sure you can deliver the presentation within the time available. As a guide, add 25 per cent to the time taken in rehearsal.
- Write for speaking, not for reading. Be careful to ensure smooth flow which matches your preferred style of delivery.
- Avoid jargon.
- Use humour to enliven the presentation where appropriate, but do so with care – it can easily backfire.
- Illustrations will emphasise your key points, improving both understanding and recall.

STAGE FOUR

Making Your Sales Presentation

'IT'S NOT because things are difficult that we do not dare. It's because we do not dare that things are difficult.'

Robert M. Hand

'NOTHING in the world can take the place of persistence . . . Persistence and determination alone are important.'

Calvin Coolidge

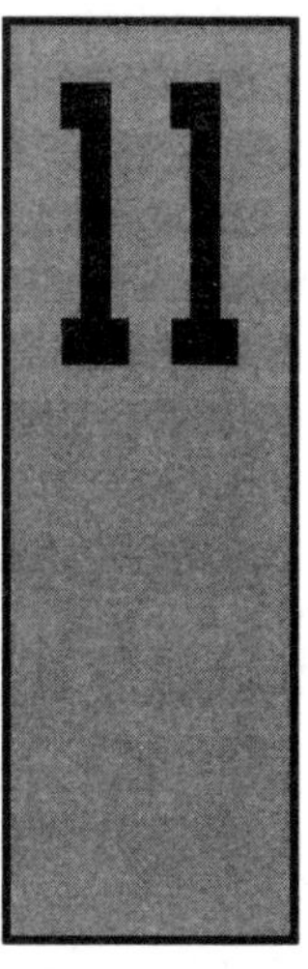

PUTTING IT ACROSS

'STRIVE to emulate the swan. Serene and calm on the surface but paddling like hell just below the water line!'

Anonymous

SINCE NO successful sales presentations can be read from a script, you have only two alternatives.

Either your pitch is impromptu or you must repeat it from memory using only the briefest of reminders.

While off-the-cuff presentations can be very effective if delivered by experienced sales professionals, there is always a risk of losing your thread or forgetting key sales points.

If you are made even slightly anxious by the prospect of presenting before an audience, a carefully written script which you have memorised and rehearsed is essential.

But this does not mean standing up and spouting some

rote-learned material in a boring and unconvincing manner.

Rather, it involves reducing your script to a series of bullet points and using these, plus your memory of the original material, to deliver a pitch which combines the confidence of a prepared text with the informality of a spontaneous sales presentation.

Here's how to set about it.

Preparing Your Presentation

Putting Variety into Your Voice

To hold your audience's attention, it is essential to put variety into your voice by changing your speed, pitch and volume. Never mumble away in a monotone.

- A deeper tone signals more confidence than a high-pitched tone.
- Rapid speech encourages shallow breathing, which increases your anxiety.
- Slow down and drop your voice to signal that you are about to make a point of great interest and importance. Pause, make eye-contact with key members of the audience.

To ensure variety and achieve the right emphasis read your script aloud and tape the results.

Replay the recording listening with care for the following points. If possible ask some disinterested third parties to offer constructive criticism. Ask them these questions:

- Am I speaking too rapidly to be clearly understood or too slowly to hold the audience's attention?
- Am I enunciating my words clearly, especially those names or technical terms that are difficult to catch?
- Am I speaking so loudly my audience will begin to feel intimidated or so softly those at the back will find it hard to catch my words?

Note those parts of the presentation where you did the following.

- Speeded up or slowed down to good effect, because your change of pace helped to emphasise a key point or move the presentation swiftly to a second benefit.
- Raised or lowered your pitch in a way which made the delivery more interesting and comprehensible. Changes in pitch are essential to avoid the monotonous delivery of some speakers who use an unvarying drone which makes it almost impossible for your audience to pay attention.
- Spoke more loudly or softly, again in such a way that it helped draw out the meaning of your words.
- Paused in order verbally to underline a particularly significant part of your presentation.

When satisfied with your presentational style mark the script, using the special notation shown below, as a guide to how it should be delivered.

↑ My voice rises
↓ My voice falls
< I speak louder
> I speak softer
// Take a short pause here
/ Take a longer pause here
∩ Tie these phrases together for a smoother flow

Here's how the inaugural speech made by US President John F. Kennedy, delivered in January 1961, looks when notated according to the way in which it was delivered.

‘And ↑so,/my ↓fellow Americans/<Ask ↑not//what your country/can do for you//>Ask what you can do/for your ↓country//’

Read your script aloud several more times to practise getting your speech patterns right.

Transferring Your Script to Prompt Cards

Write or type key points from your script on to small cards. The 3 × 5 in index size which can easily be carried in the pocket and held in the hand are most suitable.

If printing the text, use a larger typeface with double or even triple spacing.

Avoid abbreviations which may cause confusion.

Use no more than three or four lines on each card, with a maximum of six words in each.

Write them in large, easily seen block capitals.

An alternative to cards, used by many professional presenters, is to cue yourself via the visual aids as described in the previous chapter. Provided you have rehearsed your presentation thoroughly, the bullet points or transparencies plus brief notes on the OHP mounts will be sufficient reminders.

Go through your speech again, this time using these prompt cards to jog your memory.

Rehearsing Before a Mirror

When you feel comfortable about the words, the final stage is to get the body language right. Some professional speakers suggest that, if you own a video camera, it is helpful to tape your rehearsal. One problem is that, depending on how the picture is framed, your camera sees you in a way your audience does not.

Focus on your head and shoulders, for example, and expression and gestures will be all the camera records. Yet your listeners will be taking in your whole body, so that posture and stance are going to be important as well. It also means that your facial expression and gestures will be exaggerated in a way that will not occur during the presentation.

For these reasons I prefer a full-length mirror which shows you everything your audience will see. Even better, do your final rehearsal before an audience of friends, relatives or colleagues.

Practice Makes Perfect Team Presentations

So far I have considered the presentation from the point of view of individuals. But many large-scale sales presentations involve a team effort.

When presenting as a member of a sale team it is essential you rehearse together on at least two occasions. Your first rehearsal should be a relaxed but thorough run-through. Try a brain-storming session in which all the main points needing to be made are identified and assigned to the people who will be presenting them.

After thinking about your presentation between the first and second rehearsal, you will almost certainly come up with new ideas which should be discussed with your fellow presenters prior to the second, dress rehearsal.

This rehearsal is crucial. No matter how busy you all are time must be set aside for it.

Make certain all those who will be presenting are there. Kick around any new ideas and slot them into place.

Now go through the whole presentation, including all visuals, preferably before an audience of independent minds, either from within the company or brought in from outside.

With the help of your critics, assess the impact of your presentation. If you have recorded the presentation listen and criticise yourselves.

Rehearse The Qs and As as Well

You should also rehearse the question and answer sessions at the end of your sales presentation. Brief the invited audience to ask challenging questions. Discuss who will answer these and how best to respond to such questions. Rehearsing your Qs and As offers two benefits.

- Knowing you have your answers ready means you will not only BE but also FEEL prepared. This increases the team's self-confidence.
- When the questions come you will deal with them professionally. If they are not asked all that has been lost is a little time.

Whom to Take on a Sales Presentation

When a sales presentation is to be made by several members of the company, there may be some difficulty in deciding who should go along.

Speaking as a veteran of hundreds of successful pitches, Graham Lancaster, chairman of PR consultancy Biss Lancaster advises:

> 'Take the team you're proposing will handle the business. Clients are suspicious of top people in an agency going along and doing the pitch with their interpersonal skills, all guns blasting, and then never seeing these people again. The team who'll work on the business are those to present.'

Basil Towers, chairman and managing director of Christow Consultants, agrees.

> 'Always take people who will work on the account – every time. Play the honesty card very hard indeed for you'll probably get asked at the end of the presentation how you can guarantee that those people will work on the account. I would never take more than six people and only that many if I needed them all because the client will be overwhelmed.'

Motivating Your Selling Team

The fact that you've been asked to make the presentation is often sufficient motivation for a team to excel. Most sales people are excited by the prospect of winning new business. It's a personal challenge and one where success often provides a fast track to senior management.

Unfortunately the marketing departments of some small and medium-sized companies are sometimes dominated by a few strong personalities. These superstars never delegate and refuse to concede that anyone else can sell as well as they do. This creates a negative atmosphere which undermines confidence and increases anxiety among other sales staff.

Although this may work well for a while, the time comes when these companies either reach a size or a stage in their development where this approach become untenable or unacceptable.

If, on the other hand, your culture avoids creating prima donnas and is fully supportive of all those involved in selling you will avoid generating these handicapping concerns and anxieties.

Motivating your sales team must start right from the first rehearsal where you are brain-storming ideas. Make it a golden rule that no idea is a bad idea.

Help whoever is putting the presentation together to identify and eliminate any ideas which may not work while giving them the confidence that they understand the market. Never say: 'That's completely wrong and you'll just make a fool of yourself.'

Provide positive and constructive comments by using the PIN approach. Start by commenting on:

P = Everything *P*ositive in their proposals

I = Then move on to discuss all the *I*nteresting ideas – whether or not these seem immediately practical

N = Only then consider any *N*egative aspects of their suggestions.

By rewarding them with praise right from the start, you reduce any antagonism or anxiety aroused by more critical remarks.

'Even if someone on the team isn't fluent or is mumbling you have to be careful,' advised Bill Towers. 'You say something like "Perhaps this is a better way of putting it . . .". During the presentation, keep eye contact with whoever's speaking and nod – it's a sign of encouragement and of interest.'

After the presentation allow two or three days to pass before a debrief session as people are very hyped up and will need to unwind.

If you need to criticise them do this gently by saying something like, 'I believe we could have done some things better.'

Such an approach ensures that morale and team spirit remain high in readiness for the next group presentation.

Motivating Yourself

The three essential elements of sales success are:

- confidence
- enthusiasm
- persistence.

You have to sound and look like a winner, because people made anxious by the prospect of the change which selling implies are eager for the reassurance and encouragement which only enthusiasm and confidence can convey.

You can only do this by developing a positive mental attitude towards the challenge of winning new business. Remember:

- you are what you think you are;
- you act the way you think you are;
- you are what you are by habit;

- you develop the habit – and then the habit develops you;
- success is as much of a habit as failure;
- as you think so shall you be;
- take charge of your life.

In the words of Buddha: 'All that we are is the result of what we have thought.'

Use The Body Language Of Success

When you enter the room at the start of your presentation walk and look like a winner. The body language of success occupies a book in itself* and all sales people should be familiar with key aspects of non-verbal communication.

But here are a dozen ways to sell yourself without saying a word.

1. Move energetically and with a light step

This communicates self-confidence and enthusiasm. But be careful not to come across as brash or cocky.

2. Your handshake should be firm and dry

If you are one of those people whose palm becomes sweaty with anxiety then discreetly wipe it on a handkerchief before extending your hand.

A damp, limp grasp conveys an extremely negative message, especially when offered by one male to another.

3. Talk like a winner

Use a firm, confident – but never aggressive – manner. When addressing a group speak slightly more slowly than you would during an informal conversation with one or two others. This gives your voice greater authority and makes you sound more serious.

* See my book *The Secret Language of Success* (Bantam Books 1989).

4. Use eye-contact correctly

This is vitally important. Too much eye-contact and you will seem aggressive, too little and the message communicated is one of untrustworthiness.

During business meetings the eyes normally focus on a triangle formed by lines drawn across the bridge of the nose and down the edges of each eye. Keeping your gaze in this area conveys interest, intensity, seriousness and self-confidence.

In a relaxed, friendly encounter your gaze should shift downwards to take in the nose, lips and chin. This communicates interest and a desire to get to know the other person better.

If you are a man dealing with another male, maintain eye-contact for between 60 and 70 per cent of the time of your conversation.

Anything less may be taken as a sign of unease or lack of confidence. A longer gaze, however, will be interpreted as aggressive.

If you are a male dealing with a woman, reduce eye-contact to around 50 per cent of the exchange. But be very careful not to allow your gaze to drop below the business target triangle since this implies a desire for greater intimacy.

If you are a woman dealing with a man and you want to assert yourself in the situation, use eye-contact around 70 per cent of the time.

Should you wish silently to signal a compliant or submissive attitude, reduce the duration of gaze to about 50 per cent.

Be aware, however, that the longer period of eye-contact will communicate a strong, dominant and self-confident personality which some men may find disturbing and stressful. Where it is important to assert your authority, the longer gaze is necessary. When you are more concerned with gaining co-operation you should reduce the amount of eye-contact.

If you are a woman talking to another woman, then maintain eye-contact for around 70 per cent of the time. This should not normally arouse any discomfort.

Be careful, however, to keep your eyes on the target triangle. Women unused to dealing with assertive, confident females may interpret a longer gaze as a threat.

5. Give eye-contact when the other person *starts* talking

This signals that you are not only paying attention but find what is being said of great interest. Use any pauses in their speech to break eye-contact.

Look away briefly just before replying, since this sends out a message of a thoughtful and considered response. Return gaze while speaking, using natural pauses in your dialogue to shift gaze momentarily. When you have reached the end of your remarks, glance downward to signal clearly your desire for a response from the other person.

Remember that the greater attention and interest you can convey by means of appropriately used gaze, the more that other person will believe you like them and the more liking they will show you in return.

6. Look around the room

When addressing a group, move your gaze around the room so that every member of your audience feels included in the presentation. Notice how show-business professionals take in their entire audience, from stalls to gallery.

If you are shy you may have difficulty using eye-contact correctly when making a presentation.

In this case train yourself in its effective use by carrying out the following practice, first with friends, then colleagues and eventually clients.

- Relax (see Chapter 12).
- Plan a topic in advance. This helps take the edge off nervousness if you have prepared for a conversation.
- While speaking, stand or sit comfortably. If standing make sure you are evenly balanced.
- Focus your gaze on the target triangles and start talking.

With a little practice you will find giving the right amount of eye-contact comes easily and naturally.

7. Smile a lot

This has both a positive effect on your audience, and actually makes you feel happier and more confident.

8. Never stand behind a lectern or podium when speaking

This conceals a major part of your body language so preventing you from communicating those vital silent speech messages.

9. Don't fold your arms

While making your presentation stand with your hands at your sides or clasped behind your back. Never fold your arms or put your hands in your pockets when addressing an audience.

10. Use open palm gestures

Keep your elbows away from your body as this projects a warm and welcoming posture.

11. Don't clench your fists

While listening to questions keep your hands unclenched in order to communicate the fact that you trust your listeners and are trustworthy in return.

12. Try anchoring

To obtain a positive response from your customer use a powerful piece of body language known as 'anchoring'. This consists of briefly touching the other person as you speak his or her name. Repeating their name while shaking hands works up to a point, but the subconscious effect becomes more powerful when an additional touch is used, for example a light pat to the forearm. The power of this silent speech signal stems from the fact that you will have aroused positive feelings in your customer by using friendly greetings and use of their first name.

By lightly touching your customer's arm while you use his or her name, that positive emotion is 'anchored' to your presence. At a subsequent meeting you can reactivate a similarly warm response by use of the same light touch. The sequence is as follows:

> arouse positive emotion – anchor with light touch – at a later meeting, reactivation of the initial positive feeling is achieved by repeating this sequence – light touch – positive feelings aroused – positive feelings associated with your presence.

The handshake works less well as an anchor because it's something we do so often and with such a wide range of people, some of them liked and admired, others probably disliked even despised, so no particularly warm emotion attaches to the action. An anchoring touch, by being unusual, provides a more powerful trigger. But be careful about where and how the other person is touched, by following the advice given below.

For anchoring to be successful it must be used within a framework of reassuring body language and positive emotions. Having their name remembered by a salesperson who seems angry, anxious or uninterested is hardly going to make customers feel good about either themselves – or you!

TWENTY WAYS TO DITCH YOUR PITCH

1. Talk too rapidly or too slowly
2. Speak monotonously
3. Use too high a vocal pitch

4. Talk without saying very much
5. Speak too softly
6. Show little passion or enthusiasm
7. Talk in abstract terms without providing concrete examples
8. Use needless jargon
9. Use slang or bad language
10. Talk without enough preparation or knowledge
11. Speak in a disorganised and rambling manner
12. Talk down to the audience
13. Make your audience feel stupid
14. Insult your audience's intelligence
15. Do not summarise your message
16. Refuse to make eye-contact
17. Fidget and distract your audience
18. Do not smile
19. Fail to use visual aids
20. Fail to close effectively

ACTION PLAN 13

If you have difficulty delivering a scripted speech effectively, practise with a previous presentation or create one especially for this exercise.

Use the notation described above to mark the script indicating how it should be delivered.

Analyse short sections of speeches delivered by professional speakers, such as politicians, tape recorded from radio and TV. Write out a transcript then mark in the pauses, points of emphasis etc. Decide whether that text could have been delivered more forcefully had the speech patterns been altered.

When watching speakers presenting at meetings

or on television become aware of their use of body language.

Use the log below to record key non-verbal signals used. This will help you identify and eliminate unhelpful or distracting messages from your own body language repertoire, while improving those signals which help to create a positive impression.

You should also ask friends or relatives to rate your own performance during rehearsals using the same system.

Rate each signal on a scale of 1 to 5, where 1 = very negative impression and 5 = very positive impression.

Tick the appropriate observation. You aim to achieve the maximum possible score of 35 points.

BODY LANGUAGE LOG

Message	*Rating*	*What went wrong*
SMILE		INSUFFICIENT SMILING SMILE APPEARED INSINCERE SMILED TOO MUCH
EYE-CONTACT		INSUFFICIENT EYE-CONTACT TOO MUCH – APPEARED AGGRESSIVE MADE EYE-CONTACT AT WRONG TIME
POSTURE		TOO RELAXED TOO STIFF
HANDSHAKE		TOO FIRM TOO SOFT TOO MOIST

Message	*Rating*	*What went wrong*
MOVEMENTS		TOO BRISK – APPEARED AGITATED TOO SLOW – SEEMED LETHARGIC CONVEYED ENERGY AND CONFIDENCE FIDGETED TOO MUCH
GESTURE		INSUFFICIENT TOO MUCH GESTURE – DISTRACTING
OVERALL IMPRESSION		GOOD AVERAGE POOR

KEY POINTS

- Successful sales presentations should combine the precision of a carefully prepared and rehearsed script with the informal spontaneity of an off-the-cuff delivery. Achieve this by memorising the general outlines of a scripted pitch and then extemporising around brief bullet points.
- Rehearse the script to get a smooth and effective presentation. Use a tape recorder to develop the most persuasive delivery. Use the special notation to indicate how the script can be most effectively spoken.
- Check your body language using a full-length mirror in preference to a video camera which may overemphasise some of your non-verbal messages.

- When selling as part of a team, at least two rehearsals are vital, the first to brain-storm the best approach and allocate roles, the second to ensure a smooth presentation.
- Correct use of body language is essential. Be especially careful to smile, use appropriate eye-contact, and convey an impression of confidence and energy.
- Anchoring, which involves lightly touching the customer to create positive emotions in them, is a powerful, non-verbal way of enhancing liking for you.

12 HOW TO CONTROL YOUR NERVES

'WHEN MAKING a presentation, your goal is not to remove all the butterflies from your stomach but to convince the butterflies to fly in formation.'

Vincent DiSalvo

IF YOU EXAMINE all those situations most likely to arouse anxiety, from flying to speaking in public, you'll find a single, underlying cause: the fear of losing control!

So long as we feel in command of events, master or mistress of our own destiny, challenges will be viewed as exciting rather than risky, and stimulating instead of fearful.

Research, careful scripting and adequate rehearsal will all significantly improve your sense of control over your sales presentation.

But if you are still seriously alarmed by the prospect of

public speaking, it will be useful to gain greater control over the mental and physical effects of high anxiety. These can include all or some of the following:

- rapidly beating heart;
- uneven breathing;
- dry mouth;
- upset stomach, nausea;
- profuse sweating;
- trembling;
- inability to think straight;
- loss of confidence and increasing self-doubt;
- negative thoughts such as 'I cannot cope with this situation';
- feelings of panic.

Not surprisingly, such feelings will undermine even the best-rehearsed presentation, causing the victim to mumble and stumble.

Unfortunately, because anxiety is contagious, it is quite likely the audience – sensing your acute discomfort – will become tense and uncomfortable themselves.

TEN GIVE-AWAY SIGNS OF NERVES

1. Increased eye blinks
2. Hands in pocket
3. Finger tapping
4. Faster, jerkier gestures
5. Increased rate of speaking
6. Frequent throat clearing
7. Frequent hair smoothing
8. Standing on the sides of the feet
9. Scuffing the feet
10. Licking and chewing the lips

Lesson: Even if you feel nervous try to avoid the above tell-tale signs. Without them your audience may never even guess how anxious you are.

Luckily there are a number of practical, easily mastered ways of bringing the disagreeable symptoms under control; in Victor DiSalvo's memorable phrase making the 'butterflies fly in formation'.

ALL GOOD SPEAKERS SUFFER FROM NERVES

You may derive some comfort from the fact that all effective speakers suffer presentation nerves.

When Margaret Thatcher was prime minister she was once asked whether she was ever anxious when addressing Parliament. She replied: 'I am nervous every time I go to the House of Commons. Every time I go in, I think "Now look love, keep calm. Concentrate." So as I get up, yes, I'm desperately nervous.

'Believe you me, if I go to Wimbledon or to the Cup Final, I know exactly how those people feel when they walk out on to the pitch or on to the court – nervous, frightened to death until the game starts and then they lose themselves in the game. And that's the only way to do it.'

Lesson: When controlled, anxiety helps you give a better presentation. The secret is knowing how to exercise such control.

How Presentation Anxiety Arises

Anxiety is triggered by a primitive survival mechanism, known as the 'fight/flight' response. This evolved at a time when we faced daily threats of violence and death, from wild animals and human foes.

Once this reflex takes over you are no longer capable of dealing with events in a calm and logical manner. In fact telling yourself to 'calm down' or 'keep cool' may even make matters worse. As your body continues to respond as if facing a physical threat to survival, the failure of your brain to take charge of events leads to even greater anxiety. Now the thoughts which flood into your increasingly panic-stricken mind are along the lines of 'I'm going to lose control . . .', 'I've got to get away . . .', 'I am going to make a fool of myself . . .'.

These panicky ideas cause an even stronger physical response, so generating a spiral of ever more handicapping negative thoughts and disruptive bodily reactions.

Because it was designed to aid survival in extremis the fight/flight response can function extremely swiftly.

Survival demands an immediate response. We do not have the luxury to reflect at length on how dangerous the sudden threat really is.

This is the familiar 'startle' reaction which occurs, for example, when we are suddenly scared by a loud noise.

Here's what happens to your body, together with an approximate time scale – in thousandths of a second – whenever the response is triggered.

Time Since Startle	*Response*
12 milliseconds	Your jaw muscles tighten.
16 milliseconds	Your eyes and brows contract.

Time Since Startle	*Response*
20 milliseconds	Your shoulder and neck muscles tighten, raising your shoulders and pulling your head forward.
50 milliseconds	Your elbows bend. Hands start to turn palm downward.
60 milliseconds	Your stomach muscles contract and your rib cage is drawn down, disturbing your breathing.
70 milliseconds	Your knees bend and turn inward. Your ankles roll the feet inward.
80 milliseconds	Your crotch muscles tighten. Your toes lift upward.
90 milliseconds	Your heart rate increases.
100 milliseconds	Your mouth goes dry and your digestion slows.
150 milliseconds	Your breathing becomes irregular.
200 milliseconds	Your palms start to sweat.
250 milliseconds	Your face grows pale.

In around a quarter of a second, your whole body is transformed into a condition of high physical arousal. 'It happens before we can consciously perceive it or inhibit it,' comments Dr Thomas Hanna, director of the Novato Institute for Somatic Research and Training. 'It is our primitive protector, whose motto is "Withdraw now, and think about it later".'

After this initial, high speed reaction to startle, the body can remain tense for minutes or even hours afterwards. Some chronically stressed individuals remain in an almost perpetual state of physical arousal.

But it doesn't take an unexpected sound or objective danger to trigger the fight/flight response.

Anything which is perceived as putting us at risk, and this includes the psychological threat of making a presentation, may cause this rapid increase in arousal.

Defeating the Anxiety Spiral

When anxiety is allowed to build, your concentration slips and your ability to communicate declines. Physical tension even makes your voice sound different. As I explained in Chapter 6, research has shown that a tense man sounds irritable and inflexible, while a tense woman comes across as emotional, irrational and less intelligent.

The same rapid relaxation procedure used to calm you down prior to making a challenging phone call (see page 121) can be used to reduce mental and physical stress before a sales presentation. You may find this easier to master if you first learn the longer relaxation procedure described in Action Plan Fourteen on page 249.

Fast Track Relaxer

- Sit down as comfortably as you can and loosen any tight clothing.
- Deliberately tighten your muscles. Clench your fists, try touching the backs of your wrists to your shoulders, frown and close your eyes tightly, press the tip of your tongue against the roof of your mouth, stretch your legs, point your toes, flatten your stomach and take a deep breath.
- Hold all this tension for a slow count to five.
- As you slowly exhale allow your whole body to go limp. Imagine you are a puppet whose strings have been cut. Let your shoulders drop right down and unclench your fingers as your flop down into the chair. Unfurrow your brow and let your jaw hang loose, teeth unclenched.
- Now take a second deep breath and hold for a slow count to five.

- Breathe slowly and deeply for a further fifteen seconds. Each time you breathe out repeat the word CALM ... CALM silently and feel the relaxation flowing through your whole body.
- Finally soothe your nerves by imagining yourself lying on the golden sands of a sun-warmed beach by a clear blue ocean. Create as vivid an image as possible and hold it for around thirty seconds.

Controlling Stress by Controlling Breath

Try this test. Raise your right arm and clench the fist. Notice whether, as you did so, you also held your breath. If you did, the chances are that when faced with a threat you'll also hold your breath. For example, on rising to make your sales presentation you may, unintentionally and involuntarily, hold your breath. If you do, then this unconscious action will automatically raise your level of physical arousal.

When your breathing is full and efficient your whole system is emotionally, physically and intellectually enhanced.

This is why we may describe a highly creative and successful person as being 'inspired' or having an 'inspiration'.

When the breathing is irregular or inefficient, the body is placed under needless stress and tensions which make you more vulnerable to a panic attack.

When making presentations, therefore, it is very important to breathe correctly.

Check the way you breathe

We breathe between 16,000 and 20,000 times a day, but because the action is so automatic, we seldom pay much attention to how this breath is taken. Yet the way you breathe can have a profound effect on your ability to manage stress and speak confidently during a presentation.

So it is well worth while taking a few seconds to discover how you breathe. Do this as follows, by standing up straight and placing one hand on your breastbone and the other on your abdomen, just below the rib-cage.

Breathe in and out normally.

Which hand detected most movement?

If it was the hand on your breastbone, your breathing is chest or costal.

If it was the hand on your stomach, your breathing is abdominal or diaphragmatic.

Breathing and stress

Costal breathing is done by raising the chest wall using the intercostal muscles, which are attached between each rib.

Diaphragmatic breathing is done by flattening and contracting our diaphragm, while moving the upper ribs and breastbone forward and upwards to increase chest capacity. The diaphragm is a strong, dome-shaped sheet of muscle separating the chest cavity and abdomen.

In both cases a partial vacuum is created in the chest cavity drawing air into the lungs.

If your rib-cage moves mainly outwards and upwards, your breathing is shallow and costal.

If most of the work is done by your diaphragm and the muscles forming the abdominal wall, your breathing is deep and diaphragmatic.

Diaphragmatic or abdominal breathing is most efficient since expansion and ventilation occur in the lower parts of the lung which are richest in blood.

Because we breathe like this when feeling calm and confident, diaphragmatic breathing helps promote feelings of relaxation.

Chest breathing is useful during vigorous exercise, because the air is drawn into the lungs more rapidly. Because running is part of the fight/flight response, this type of breathing is also associated with tension and anxiety. This means that chest breathing can lead to feelings of tension and anxiety.

Posture affects your breathing

For rhythmical, abdominal breathing your weight should be evenly distributed and taken through the spine and pelvis while you are seated, and through your spine and legs while standing.

When making a presentation this balance is often absent and breathing badly affected as a result. So practise standing in a 'planted' position, with your back straight – but not ramrod stiff – and the weight taken equally on both feet.

Rehearsing in Your Mind's Eye

In addition to rehearsing your presentation in real life, it may also be helpful to practise in your imagination. Research has shown that visual imagery can have a powerful effect on behaviour. If you doubt this, conjure up the following scene as vividly as possible.

Imagine holding a ripe lemon in your hand.

Now see yourself cutting off a thick, wedgy slice and taking a bite.

As the tartness of the lemon hits your taste buds, your cheeks curl and lips pucker. Allow this image to fade.

Your mouth will now be filled with saliva and you have just experienced a simple but powerful demonstration of the potency of visualisation.

Here's how to use the same effect to increase your confidence and assurance when making a sales presentation.

After relaxing physically, using either the fast track procedure described above or the longer, deeper relaxation technique explained in Action Plan Fourteen on page 249, move into your mind-soothing scene.

After spending a few moments picturing yourself lying on a warm, sunny beach (or any other suitably calming location) switch your mind to the presentation.

Picture this as vividly as you can. Observe yourself performing successfully, making all your key sales points in a clear and persuasive manner, dealing with any objections and answering questions in an authoritative and effective manner.

Try and create these scenes as clearly as possible, both hearing as well as visualising what happens. Do not worry, however, if you find this rather difficult at first. About 10 per cent of people have great difficulty in forming visual images and you may find that you do not need to have pictures in your mind provided your thoughts are clear.

Think about your goal in the present tense, as if it had already been achieved.

Practise before going to sleep and first thing each morning.

Make positive and encouraging statements about yourself.

A Quick Confidence Booster

Immediately before entering the room to make your sales presentation carry out the following procedure.

Take several deep breaths.

Now breathe normally.

With every out breath feel your mind and body becoming calmer but more alert.

Bring to mind a presentation when you were exceptionally effective and successful.

Experience again the sights and sounds of that presentation.

Feel yourself filled with energy and enthusiasm.

Joy bubbles up inside you like a bottle of freshly opened champagne.

Now go in and dazzle them!

Solving Problems with Both Sides of Your Brain

As I explained earlier, a successful sales presentation is one which captures both the hearts and minds of your prospective customers. This means it must be both logical and imaginative, and objective and intuitive.

As mentioned earlier research has shown that the right side of our brain is specialised – in the majority of people – for dreaming, fantasy and intuition. The left hemisphere is where the more logical, analytical tasks are performed.

People who are too left brained tend to be strong on intellectual analysis but weaker on intuitive understanding. Those with a more active right brain, by contrast, may be too intuitive and insufficiently objective.

A technique called Cook's Hook-up, which claims to balance the brain, has been developed by Dr Paul Denninson, a specialist in brain dominance patterns.

Many sales professionals have found it a powerful and helpful method for dealing with the problem of negative thoughts. Here's what you should do.

Remove your shoes and sit comfortably in an upright chair with your feet flat on the floor.

Place your left foot on top of your right knee.

Place your right hand on your left ankle.

Place your left hand on the ball of your left foot close to the toes.

Close your eyes and place the tip of your tongue on the roof of your mouth approximately a quarter of an inch behind your teeth.

Breathe normally and hold any negative thoughts about the forthcoming presentation in your mind for about thirty seconds. Include as many details as you can in that thought.

Now, with your eyes closed, your tongue still pressed against the hard palate and the negative thought held in your mind, place your feet flat on the floor. Raise your hands and form a steeple with the fingers, pressing them together in front of you. Hold for a further thirty seconds while breathing normally.

Now open your eyes and go about your normal activities.

According to the theory, that negative thought will be attacked and dissipated by the two sides of your brain working in perfect harmony. Try it and see!

ACTION PLAN 14

DEEP RELAXATION TRAINING

You can teach yourself to relax very deeply by following the instructions below. Before starting bear these points in mind.

- The secret of successful relaxation is *passive concentration*. That is focusing the mind on what is happening *without* trying to make it happen.
- Correct breathing is essential. Breathe continuously, without pausing between the inhaled and exhaled breath. Each time you breathe out repeat the word CALM silently to yourself.
- Sit or lie comfortably and loosen tight clothing. Some people prefer to relax in a darkened room, but this is purely a matter of choice. Try to ensure you will not be disturbed during the exercise.
- The basic idea is to first tense and then relax major muscle groups in turn. Remember the sequence by using this mnemonic: *A S*oothing *F*eeling – *M*y *B*ody *H*as *P*eace.

A – Arms and hands
Start by tensing the muscles in your forearm. Do this by extending your hands at the wrists. Bend them back, raising them from the bed or seat and feel tension build in the back of forearm. Hold for a slow count to five. Allow your hands to flop down.

Feel the tension flowing out of them and notice the difference between tension and relaxation in these muscles. Now flex your hands at the wrist. Hold for a count of five. Let your hands flop back.

Tense the biceps by attempting to touch the *back* of your wrists to your shoulders. As before hold for a slow count to five before allowing them to drop limply back.

Tense the triceps by stretching your arms out as straight as possible. Hold to five. Let your arms flop down by your sides.

S – Shoulders and neck
Shrug your shoulders as hard as you can. At the same time press the head back against some firm support. Count to five. Let your shoulders drop and go limp.

F – Face
Open your eyes wide as though enquiring. Frown deeply. Screw up your eyes. Hold for five seconds. Relax. Let the lids rest lightly together. Smooth out your brow.

M – Mouth
Press tip of tongue to roof of mouth. Hold for a slow count to five. Relax and let your tongue rest loosely in your mouth. Clench your jaw firmly. Hold and relax.

B – Body
Take and hold a deep breath. Flatten your abdominal muscles as though anticipating a blow. Hold to five.

Let all your muscles go limp.

Expel air with a gasp before returning to smooth, continuous breathing.

Silently repeat the word CALM with each exhaled breath. Feel the relaxation deepening as your body feels warmer and heavier.

H – Hips, thighs, calves

Stretch your legs, toes pointed and squeeze your buttocks together. Once more, hold for a slow count to five. Relax and let the muscles flop out.

P – Picture

Having relaxed physically the next step is to conjure up a soothing mental image using the visualisation technique described above which will help calm the mind. I shall be discussing this in a moment.

After a session always stand up slowly and carry the feelings of relaxation through into your next activity.

ACTION PLAN 15

Having learned to relax when sitting or lying, you can easily carry those comfortable feelings into everyday life by using a procedure called differential relaxation. This means ensuring that all those muscles which do not need to be under tension, such as the ones in your forehead or shoulders, remain relaxed.

As you stand up after a relaxation session, notice any tense muscles and, unless this tension is serving a useful function, allow them to unwind again.

Focus on your breathing, breathing deeply and easily, breathing relaxation into your body and breathing away tension . . . breathing relaxation into your mind and breathing away any thoughts . . . scan your body and find any areas that are holding tension . . . breathe into those areas. As you exhale release the tension.

KEY POINTS

- Anxiety is a natural response to the challenge of making a sales presentation. But if it is allowed to get out of hand your performance will suffer.
- Use the sixty-second relaxation technique to calm you down physically prior to the presentation. It is easier to relax rapidly if you have already mastered deep relaxation.
- Visualising yourself presenting confidently and successfully is very helpful.
- Energise yourself by recalling a recent sales success immediately prior to your new presentation.

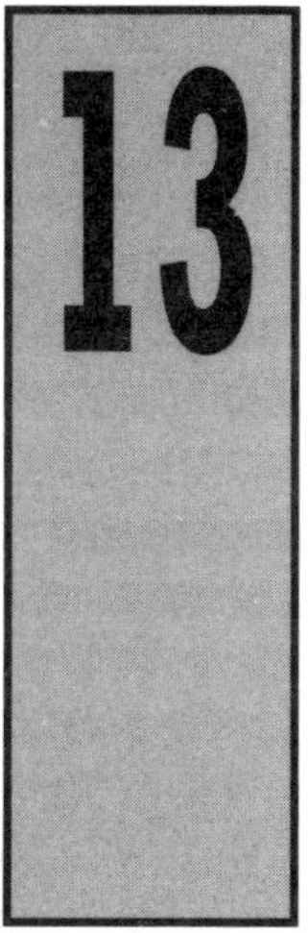

13 CREATING THE RIGHT IMPRESSION

'WHY DOES everyone take an instant dislike to me, Hawkeye?'
'Because it saves so much time, Frank.'
Exchange from the TV series M.A.S.H.

THE MOMENT of truth has arrived! In a few moments you will be making your sales presentation. You may have anywhere from sixty seconds to sixty minutes to persuade those prospective customers that they should buy from you rather than your many competitors.

Clearly, in a very brief presentation you can do little more than recite one key benefit in as coherent a manner as possible. If you succeed in arousing their interest that one-minute time slot may be extended considerably and you must be fully prepared to follow up that advantage.

But here I am mainly concerned with presentations

lasting fifteen minutes or longer. In such presentations you will be able to follow the advice the King gave Alice and 'Begin at the beginning, and go on until you come to the end: then stop'.

For the sake of convenience I have divided such presentations into three parts:

- launching
- legwork
- leaving.

Launching

When the goods on offer are equally attractive products and sales presentations equally persuasive, new business is most likely to be won by the salesperson who gives the most favourable impression. Indeed, being well liked can even compensate for a slightly less satisfactory product or presentation. As I have emphasised elsewhere in this book, buyers are increasingly seeking partnerships with their vendors. They want team players and suppliers who are regarded as being on their side. And the more effectively you create this impression the greater your chances of success.

How long do you have to make such an impression?

Studies suggest your ability to win new business may depend on what you do and say during the *first four minutes* of a first meeting with your buyer.

'That first meeting is the key meeting. The clients instantly assess you when you walk through the door,' says Basil Towers, chairman and managing director of Christow Consultants. 'It all comes down to chemistry – whether the client thinks he or she can work with you.'

While it may not be strictly true that you 'never get a second chance to make a first impression', it is certainly difficult to overcome an initially unfavourable judgement. This is because first impressions tend to be resistant to change. Rather than alter our opinions we unconsciously edit out fresh information which contradicts our initial judgement.

Having concluded that a potential supplier is unsuitable, for example, the customer is likely to pay closer attention to anything which supports this view than to any contradictory evidence.

The secret of making a favourable impression is to manage it and to remain in psychological control so that everything you say and do contributes towards a positive evaluation.

The Art of Impression Management

If asked what sort of impression they want to make on a client, most salespeople will reply in astonishment: 'A favourable one of course!'

But what you regard as a 'favourable' impression may seem quite the opposite to your prospect.

I remember chatting to a marketing specialist immediately after he had pitched for a lucrative contract: 'I am sure they were impressed,' he told me confidently.'The chairman had all kinds of ideas and I agreed with every one!'

But when, later that day, I talked to the chairman he dismissed the man's chances with a sneer. 'I could never work with such a yes man. He didn't seem to have any ideas of his own, just went along with whatever I suggested.'

On another occasion, a psychologist had been pitching to run stress management workshops for a major London bank. 'The head of personnel was a tough character,' he commented. 'But I didn't let him intimidate me. I stood up to him and argued my corner.'

He too failed to win the business. Later I learned the main obstacle had been his handling of a senior manager. 'He is obviously expert in his field,' an executive told me. 'But he raised so many objections we just could not see him as a team player.'

So if you can't be certain to succeed by either agreeing or disagreeing, what does it take? What is really meant by that deceptively simple phrase the 'favourable impression'?

Essentially, it means matching the impression you create to the expectations of whoever makes the decision to buy.

This involves not only being able to project positive qualities, but also to match what you are able to offer with those benefits the client is seeking from you as a preferred supplier.

Suppose that, among your many interpersonal skills, are those of being humorous, quick-witted, articulate, reliable, confident, meticulous, reflective, empathic and self-deprecating.

With one client, the ability to think on your feet, respond swiftly to verbal challenges and express yourself clearly could be extremely compelling benefits. This is especially likely where he, or she, has similar abilities.

Because your verbal/intellectual styles match, you are more likely to be viewed favourably.

If, on the other hand, you were to emphasise your reflective qualities, this might create an impression of somebody who was slightly too slow and plodding to be much fun to work with. With a different client, however, these could be the very points you need to stress in order to create a favourable impression.

What is involved here is neither acting a role nor pretending to be somebody you are not.

Impression management simply means responding sensitively to the demands of a particular situation. Only in this way will you be sure that every stage of the presentation is tailored to the needs of your prospective customer.

The first things to take into account are your surroundings. The rule here is to blend in with your environment and to convey the impression that you belong in that company, that you are already a team player. While you can occasionally benefit from violating the customer's expectations the safest approach is to look and act like those around you.

Clearly, behaviour and dress suitable for one type of presentation will be inappropriate for others. You would, for example, want to present a different image if addressing bankers in the board room than when talking to engineers on the factory shop floor. You must also take into account the company dress code. Many financial institutions, for example, expect formal clothes while some software houses are far more relaxed. If in doubt, include this as part of your research. Ask those who work for the organisation what is appropriate or stand outside the company premises as management leave and observe their appearance.

If in doubt play safe. Where dress is concerned, for example, I am a great believer in a conservative look, especially for making sales presentations to the senior management of major companies. Dress like a consultant rather than 'merely' a salesperson. Wear clothes that give you an air of authority and professionalism.

A grey or dark blue business suit with a plain shirt or blouse conveys a sense of professionalism.

Men should avoid bold stripes on either shirts or ties. Black shoes with plain socks are safest.

Women should wear sensible shoes and avoid anything low cut or too tight.

Attention should also be paid to grooming. Your hair needs to look trim, clean and not overly long. Clean-shaven males must ensure their shave is close.

Fingernails should be neatly trimmed and clean.

Jewellery, apart from a wedding ring, is best avoided by men while women should avoid anything too flashy. At best it may prove distracting and at worst you could give the impression of either not being very professional or very trustworthy.

While these points may seem to be trivial, research has shown that physical appearance plays a major role in the way we make up our minds about another. I have also known company executives who rejected otherwise excellent pitches purely because they disliked the appearance of the sales presenters.

One CEO of a giant multinational refused to award a major contract to a supplier because, on shaking hands with the salesman, he noticed the man's fingernails were broken and dirty: 'If he can't take trouble over personal grooming,' this executive told me, 'why should I believe that he will take trouble in his dealings with my company?'

Illogical? Of course! But the majority of our judgements about others are based on equally stereotyped and irrational assumptions.

Once the presentation has got under way it's often desirable to dispense with some degree of formality, by removing your jacket or loosening your tie.

Peter Bingle, managing director of Westminster Strategy, says that as their pitch gets going, 'Off come the jackets and you try to involve people immediately. We do that to overcome the formality of the occasion and make it as relaxed as possible. If we go in with three pin-striped suits on our side and three on theirs, it's very difficult to get some humour and an informal atmosphere going.'

Another important aspect of impression management, using body language to convey enthusiasm, energy and confidence was discussed in Chapter 12.

Both body language and speech must be brought into play in order to satisfy the second rule of effective impression management, matching your status and self-esteem to that of the customer.

The importance of creating such a match has been demonstrated experimentally by two American psychologists, Jay Hewitt and Richard Abloff.

After assessing self-esteem using a questionnaire they asked the volunteers to choose as a companion people with higher or lower levels of esteem than themselves. Those most often chosen were individuals with self-esteem equal to their own.

To make a favourable impression on a customer of low status and self-esteem it is unwise to create the impression of being extremely confident or dominant.

Managers with high status and self-esteem, on the other hand, feel less threatened when their views are challenged, always provided you possess greater expertise and make your points in a tactful manner. Indeed, they often despise those who appear lacking in confidence and authority.

This is because among the benefits they seek from doing business with a good team player is reassurance that you are capable of delivering the promised goods or services efficiently. They want someone able and willing to offer professional advice, not a 'yes person' eager to agree with anything to close the sale.

The most difficult customers are those with moderate levels of status and self-esteem, since the prospect of change is more likely to be seen as a threat than an opportunity.

Since, as I explained in Part Three, winning new business means *actively initiating change* your presentation, unless correctly handled, is liable to arouse anxiety and even antagonism.

Like those with low self-esteem they will need to be reassured and subtly flattered.

Bolster their confidence by never directly opposing or contradicting them, no matter how foolish their observations or unworkable their schemes. Instead, steer them tactfully in the right direction and then imply your ideas originated from them.

By allowing them to take at least some of the credit for your proposals their anxiety and resentment will be diminished.

See Action Plan Sixteen for practical ways of determining a person's true status and self-esteem within an organisation.

Being Noticed

When a Texan, who was also a great animal lover, bought his daughter a pony he was determined that it should be trained using only kindness. He searched Texas for a trainer with a reputation for gentleness and asked him to take on the task. On meeting the pony for the first time, the trainer gave the startled animal a brisk slap on the flanks.

'I was told you only used kindness to train animals,' fumed the furious owner.

'I do,' agreed the trainer. 'But first I got to attract their attention!'

Attracting the attention of your audience is a number one challenge at the start of your presentation and some presenters resort to startling tactics in order to achieve this goal.

Victor 'I bought the company' Kiam recalls how, on one occasion, when faced with a tough sales presentation, he literally resorted to monkey business to grab his audience's attention.

His challenge was persuading cynical buyers from America's largest wholesalers to stock Pepsodent – then number two in the toothpaste sales league – in their drugstores and supermarkets. Victor knew that they could see little difference between the various brands and didn't really care. In their view toothpaste was toothpaste.

The night before his sales presentation Victor lay awake pondering on the task. But it was not until the following morning as he passed a pet shop on his way to the presentation that Victor hit upon a bold idea for making an unforgettable pitch. Going into the shop he bought a pet monkey.

By the time Victor was called into the conference room many salespeople had made their pitch ahead of him. The buyers were bored, battle weary and unresponsive.

Taking the monkey from its cage Victor swung the animal on to his shoulders, strode into the room, placed his samples on the table and announced: 'Gentlemen, I'm here for Pepsodent and I have a monkey on my back. It's time I got him off!'

With that he let the animal race across the conference table, scattering papers, knocking over glasses and generally creating mayhem. Some of the managers went pale with fright, but the majority roared at this unexpected performance.

Victor recaptured his monkey, thanked them and left without explaining his bizarre actions or making any attempt to sell Pepsodent.

Word of his performance rapidly spread around the stores giving Pepsodent such a high profile that it soared to victory in the toothpaste race.

This bold gimmick worked wonders for him. But it could just as easily have badly misfired. This is one reason why most seasoned sales professionals have their own horror stories about attention grabbing ideas which went badly awry (see Box).

OVER AND OUT

Denis Horton recalls the occasion when, while working at United Biscuits, they launched a chocolate bar called 54321. 'We'd got the salespeople in from all over the region.

'It was a multimedia presentation and we were using a gimmick – a robot. This came on under its own steam and was operated by a man at the back of the hall.

'The robot then appeared to interact with the audience and was responsible for presenting the sales points via an interchange with the presenter. Sound was transmitted through the robot, which was quite unusual at the time.

'The robot came on and snagged on the carpet, tottered around a bit and then fell over with a crash. Smoke was coming out of it. It had worked perfectly in rehearsal but we didn't have a contingency plan, so that was the end of the presentation.'

Lesson: The KISS rule – keep it simple and straighforward – applies to gimmicks as much as scripts.

The risks of mechanical breakdown apart, even gimmicks which work perfectly can create a barrier between you and your audience. It is far better to make an impact by being professional than by depending on gadgetry.

After all, you are asking your client to put their business in your hands, which means it is your image that really matters.

The Opening Moments

When the time comes to speak, keep these six points in mind.

1. Stand up if possible. We pay more attention to people speaking when standing up than while seated. If necessary make an excuse to stand, for example by handing around notes.
2. Before speaking smile and look around at your audience, making brief eye-contact with several of them. If you know some of those present begin by looking at them. This will help put you at ease.

   When presenting to strangers select someone who looks attentive and sympathetic, then deliver your opening remarks to that person.
3. While speaking adopt a 'planted' position by keeping your feet slightly apart and flat on the floor as if you were growing out of the carpet. After moving always plant yourself again.
4. Hold up any props you are using while talking about them to ensure every member of the audience has a clear view.

   Use the hand closest to the table on which your props are placed to pick them up. Never reach across your body with the opposite arm, as this forces you to turn your back on the audience.

4. When not using your hands have them behind your back or by your side. Never put them in your pockets and try not to fidget since this is distracting and betrays a lack of confidence.
5. Always start on an upbeat note. People would far rather deal with a positive person who sounds as though he or she knows how to get things done.
6. Create word pictures. Encourage your audience to view the scene you are painting through their own eyes by using such phrases as 'What would you do if . . .', 'Assume you are . . .', 'Imagine you have just . . .'.

Legwork

Once your presentation is under way, the crucial elements you need to convey are competence, knowledge and enthusiasm.

The first two clearly derive from your experience and preparation.

Enthusiasm however, is a quality which stems from your outlook on life and attitudes towards selling. Its importance in winning new business should never be underestimated.

Henry Ford claimed:

> 'You can do anything if you have enthusiasm. Enthusiasm is the yeast that makes your hope rise to the stars.
>
> 'Enthusiasm is the sparkle in your eye, it is the swing in your gait, the grip of your hand, the irresistible surge of your will and your energy to execute your ideas. Enthusiasts are fighters. They have fortitude. They have staying qualities. Enthusiasm is at the bottom of all progress! With it there is accomplishment. Without it there are only abilities.'

B.C. Forbes, millionaire businessman and founder of *Forbes* magazine, proclaimed that:

> 'Enthusiasm is the all-essential human jet propeller. White heat enthusiasm can melt the hardest problems ... It begets boldness, courage, kindles confidence, overcomes doubts, creates energy, the source of all accomplishment.'

Enthusiasm then, may be described as joyous excitement. This burning desire to accomplish your sales goal can only be generated through a genuine belief in both yourself and what you are selling. Only the truly persuaded can really persuade.

To sustain enthusiasm in the face of set-backs is seldom easy, but provided you keep these three points in mind it becomes as easy as ABC.

A = Act animated. The nineteenth-century psychologist William James pointed out that acting and feelings go together. You can act as you want to and this tends to make you feel as you want to.

B = Believe in the benefits you are offering. Remember you can only sell something you are already sold on.

C = Create an inner excitement by making the confidence-boosting statement 'I can and will accomplish my sales goal today' six times prior to your presentation. Incorporate similar positive affirmations into the visualisation exercise described in Chapter 12.

How to Handle Objections

Where possible objections should be pre-empted through anticipation and thorough research. Once somebody has raised an objection it is harder to persuade them to change their minds. Try and provide 'yessable ...' options at every stage of your presentation.

The chances of objections being raised can also be lessened by the way in which you deal with potentially contentious issues.

Present only your side of the situation if your audience:

1. already favours your proposals;
2. lacks in-depth knowledge of the subject;

3. is unlikely to be exposed to counter arguments.

Give both sides of the situation when your audience:

1. opposes your proposals;
2. knows as much or more than you do about the subject;
3. will be exposed to counter arguments.

While fairly and clearly presenting both sides of the argument, also explain the reasoning that led to you adopting a particular view of the matter. Such openness will make you seem more, not less, credible and trustworthy.

When objections are raised you should respond without ever directly contradicting the client, since this is likely to strengthen their objection. Instead help them recognise that an alternative viewpoint exists which can be equally valid.

The main points to bear in mind are as follows.

- Never define the objection as a problem or difficulty. Use a neutral term, such as 'the issue you have raised . . .' or 'the point you make . . .'.
- Congratulate them on raising the point (this helps prevent the objection becoming more deeply entrenched), but explain you have already thought of it. Say this even if the idea would never have occurred to you in a million years. 'The point you make is a good one. We took this issue into account when preparing . . .'.
- Rephrase your customer's objection in your own words. This has two positive consequences. First, it depersonalises the objection and places it more in the public domain. So long as they regard an objection as their own personal property, people are more likely to defend it to the death. Second, it prevents them from claiming, after you have responded, that you had not fully understood their concerns. So rephrase and demand confirmation that you have fully comprehended the point being made.
- Ask if there are any further points they would like to raise. This saves you from an unending barrage of subsequent

objections. Some people never seem to contribute anything to meetings except endless disagreement.

- Respond to the point in the most positive and persuasive way possible. 'Your views (concerns etc.) are, I know, shared by many people. Yet what our clients have found after using this product/service is that ...'

One frequent objection to changing suppliers is based on loyalty to the previous vendors: 'We have always dealt with X and found their services very satisfactory. Why should we give it to your company?'

There is no instant way to gain the level of confidence your rival has developed with the client, nor should you ever attack their competence or reliability.

To do so will generally provoke defensive attack, partly out of 'loyalty' to a respected supplier but also because of the implication that if the first supplier is as duff as you say they are, the executive to whom you are pitching must be stupid or ignorant to have gone on using their services.

A safer approach is to praise your rivals, while raising a realistic doubt in the client's mind as to their ability to satisfy current needs.

'Yes, I know them well, they are an excellent company which has done good work for you in the past. But because this is such a new project you might feel that bringing fresh minds to bear on the problems would be helpful. After all there is truth in the old saying about onlookers seeing more of the game than players.'

This 'Yes ... but' combination is a powerful way of simultaneously praising and raising doubts.

How to Handle Cynicism and Sarcasm

If you are already feeling apprehensive, cynical or sarcastic comments may undermine your self-confidence to the point where your presentation starts unwinding. Be prepared to deal with such a response confidently and correctly as follows:

- never rise to the bait or lose your temper;
- keep your sense of humour;
- regard rudeness as an expression of that individual's approach to business and life rather than a reflection of company policy;
- duck, dive and move on.

Dealing with Mistakes

There are five basic blunders which salespeople must always avoid.

1. Never arrive late. Assume cars will break down, trains be delayed and flights cancelled every time you set off to make a sales presentation (see Box).

   Arrive well in advance of the appointed time, even if this means waiting outside in your car. Use such time to boost your sales confidence with positive affirmations.

TRANSPORTS OF DELIGHT?

'It was our first pitch as a new agency,' recalls Paul Cowan. 'We were about five weeks old and had been invited to pitch for the Ideal Home Exhibition advertising account. It wasn't an enormous amount of business but we took it very seriously – probably too seriously. We took absolutely everybody with us – the pitching team was far too large and we'd produced far too much material in our enthusiasm to win the business.

'The meeting was to take place at their office, and being a new agency we decided to economise and go by tube. We thought we knew where we were going – and got off at what seemed to be the right station. Unfortunately, it was only then that we realised we were supposed to be at another station about two miles away.

'There was no taxi rank and no taxis passing.

'I borrowed £20 from one of the team and stood in the middle of the road. When a builder's van came along I flagged it down with two £10 notes.

'Everybody piled in the back and squatted on the bags of cement. We turned up at the client's door covered in dust. It was the funniest pitch we ever did and the fact we didn't get the business didn't matter.'

2. Avoid going for glitz and coming across as superficial. Your ideas must have depth and conviction. Some salespeople promise the world and then fail to deliver. They seldom get a second chance.
3. Never outstay your welcome. If offered one hour for your sales presentation, complete it – including questions and answers – within those sixty minutes.
4. If you bring in a team every member must contribute and not just be there for effect or to make up numbers.
5. Never seem arrogant by giving the impression you are bound to win the business because you represent a major company or have the balance of power in the transaction.

These avoidable errors apart, mistakes will still occur, no matter how carefully you have prepared and rehearsed your presentation.

The great thing is not to lose your nerve or allow that set-back to damage your confidence. This is sometimes easier said than done!

Mistake one: missing the target

Even the best-prepared presentations sometimes misfire and it can be a nerve-racking experience to discover that, despite all the hard work, your pitch is falling on very stony ground.

Basil Towers recalls a time, many years ago, when he was involved in a presentation to British Steel: 'There were eight of them on one side of the table and fourteen of us on our side – the biggest pitching team I've ever been on. But it became increasingly obvious that the whole of our presentation was angled wrongly.

'Instead of dancing on our feet and rejigging it, we laboured on and on.

'You could see their eyes closing. It was a complete disaster.'

Saving the day

Be honest when you blunder. 'I once pitched to Southern Electricity,' says Basil Towers. 'It was blatantly obvious after five minutes that we were going on the wrong track. So I stopped and said: "Look, what I think you want to hear about is this and this. What we have come to talk about is this . . ."

'We completely turned it round and we won the business. They were impressed we had the guts to say that and the ability to think on our feet. We busked it and that was the main reason they picked us over and above four other agencies. It's all down to experience and confidence.'

If you are off-target follow this example and admit the fact rather than pressing on regardless. As a wise old oilman once remarked: 'If you haven't struck oil after ten minutes stop boring!'

Try turning the presentation around. You cannot do any worse and may even impress the customer with this display of courage, decisiveness and quick thinking.

But the best way is to avoid that mistake entirely by always telling your audience what *they* want to hear, not what *you* think they ought to want to hear!

Mistake two: human error

Paul Cowan remembers pitching for part of the Leyland account, when the firm he then worked for already had a major share of their business:

'The presentation was being done on slides and the slides were sorted into carousels. We'd worked all night on the presentation, putting in loads of ideas, and I was very tired. Just as we were about to start, I picked up two carousels to put them on to the projector. But I hadn't screwed on one of the lids properly.

'The carousel fell from my hands and in an effort to stop it I dropped the other as well. The result was 120 slides scattered across the Leyland board room.

'All I could think to say was: "You've seen the work, what do you think of it?" It took me thirty minutes to put the slides back together and we didn't get the business.'

Saving the day

Tiredness and apprehension increase the chances of mistakes by reducing your span of attention and powers of concentration. On their own they are a hazard, together they can lead to major mistakes.

The more time you can allow yourself to perform even simple actions, the easier it is to avoid silly mistakes. Never make assumptions about anything. Assumptions are the mother of all cock-ups.

Mistake three: gremlins in the works

The higher tech your presentations the greater the likelihood of getting gremlins in the works, as the following case history illustrates.

An advertising executive, who prefers to remain anonymous, remembers the occasion when his agency was pitching for the £8 million business of an international toy company. Presentations, by competing agencies, were held in

Paris in front of the company's senior executives who had been flown in from all over the world.

'We were using projectors linked to a sound tape – the voiceover had pulses which stimulated the projectors to change the slides.

'It was pretty high-tech stuff and we wanted to keep the equipment with us at all times. We'd taken it on the plane and cleared it through Customs as hand luggage. The significance of this didn't strike me until much later. We got to the hotel and found everyone was sitting around the edge of this enormous ballroom.

'I was thinking: "It won't be a problem, it'll come to me, I've done it a thousand times."

'The first presentation was made and a second. Then it was my turn. At that point I realised the previous team had dimmed the lights at one end of the ballroom in order to see our slides. This left me in virtual darkness.

'So I decided to move into the light and establish some rapport with the audience. However, the PA system was faulty, and they couldn't hear me unless I stuck the microphone horizontally across my mouth, which covered my nose and just left my eyes showing over the top!

'I could hear silences between my sentences – and they were getting longer. Then I realised I was getting stage fright in the most serious way possible and was drying up.

'I noticed my legs felt incredibly heavy. I could hear myself breathing and the perspiration was breaking out on my brow.

'I could see the worried looks on our team's faces. Even the clients appeared concerned. It was all going horribly wrong.

'Luckily, in advertising you always have a parachute – showing your work. It will buy you thirty seconds. You say, "In case I haven't made that clear enough I will show you what I mean," and hold up a chart, for example. Somehow I managed to say those words, unglued my feet from the floor and moved towards the projector. I pushed the button and heaved a great sigh of relief, thinking my troubles were over.

'But all I could see were the projectors going demented. In four seconds, they had discharged their entire contents in a floor show which would have been a delight to any rave, while the sound track burbled on.

'I had managed to wipe the pulses off the voiceover by going through the Customs X-ray machine, so all the slides had cascaded through at once.'

Saving the day

Because technology is so prone to gremlins some sales professionals prefer to avoid it entirely. They argue that the moment you darken the room to show slides, for instance, eye-contact with the customer stops and your audience drifts off into their own little world.

Despite frequent horror stories I still believe in the tremendous persuasive power of the images of visual aids when making a major sales presentation.

In my view the main lesson to be learned from technical snafus is the importance of checking every detail, no matter how small and apparently insignificant. Indeed, it is often the small details which cause the biggest mistakes.

Instead of relying on memory, prepare a detailed checklist covering every contingency and work your way through it like a pilot doing pre-flight checks.

If all else fails try humour. Advertising executive Charlie Makin recalls presenting to a major manufacturer when the bulb went on his overhead projector: 'I ran across and switched on the back-up bulb. Nobody had noticed there was a problem – until the second bulb went five minutes later.

'So I said: "Obviously God doesn't want us to win this business." Everybody laughed and I carried on talking and kept the whole thing going.'

Most mistakes are recoverable through a combination of honesty, humour and quick thinking. Occasionally, however, something goes wrong from which it is very hard to see how any recovery can be possible.

One such catastrophe occurred when an account director

called to make a presentation at his client's offices. He had brought his own equipment with him, a heavy back-projection slide unit with a carousel on top.

His client was waiting in reception to greet him. To shake hands he swung the audio-visual equipment out of the way. Unfortunately, it swung back too far, and struck the client so hard one of his legs fractured.

While the receptionist called the ambulance, the horrified account director could only murmur: 'I think I'd better just go, I don't think I'm of any help to you at all.'

Under the circumstances it's hard to see what else he could say!

The Body Language of Buying

Textbooks on selling advise salespeople to apply the ABC – always be closing – principle throughout their presentations.

In many ways this is sound advice. One can certainly talk a prospect *out* of closing the deal if you rabbit on too long. Once they have been persuaded to buy, then all further discussion is unnecessary and probably unhelpful.

None the less, by becoming aware of the silent speech messages which people send out when ready to buy you can time your closes more precisely, thereby increasing the likelihood of success.

Reading the buy signs

Here are the major silent speech signals which reveal the moment when your customer is ready to buy.

1. Relaxation

As they make up their mind to buy people often grow more relaxed.

2. Closer proximity

A customer ready to buy usually moves closer to you when standing or leans forward in their chair when seated.

4. Increased eye-contact
Once a buying decision has been made the customer's gaze becomes longer and more frequent.

5. Chin touch
When ready to buy some customers will briefly touch their chin. Why this should happen is not known and it is a less frequent and reliable sign that the others. But if you spot it when presenting, immediately move to a trial close.

Leaving

'I find the most powerful bit of the presentation is that last minute', says Basil Towers. 'If you get it right, you will leave the client feeling you are hungry, keen, the people for the job and anxious to get on with it as soon as possible.'

Create this last and lasting impression by restating key aspects of your presentation. If using a projector make sure the final slide emphasises these points.

People recall best what they hear first and last, so it is essential your closing remarks carry a great deal of relevance and punch. Never allow the sales presentation simply to tail off into silence.

Having dealt with all the points you intended, your last task is to invite questions. This should never be regarded as a formality. On the quality of your answers may depend whether or not you win the business. Even a less than perfect presentation can sometimes be saved by a cracking Q and A session. It's one final chance to demonstrate your ability to think on your feet while conveying enthusiasm, energy and good ideas.

Handling Questions and Answers

These can prove extremely stressful if you find it hard to think on your feet. When handled effectively, however, Q and A sessions can prove an ideal opportunity to:

- underline your key points;
- clear up misunderstandings;
- accentuate the positive aspects of your product or service, those unique benefits that will win you the new business.

Here are six ways to handle even the toughest questions.

1. 'We've found our current suppliers, the XYZ company really lousy on their delivery times. What do you think of them?' If your customer makes negative comments about competitors, listen carefully in order to learn all you can but never criticise them yourself. Keep the focus on your strengths rather than a rival's alleged weaknesses. Respond along the lines, 'That's a problem you'd have to take up with them directly of course. They do have a good reputation, although I believe our computerised delivery system is superior. In fact we've built our business by making promises and keeping them.'
2. Always pause for four seconds (count 'one-and-two-and-three-and-four') before responding to a question. This shows you care about what has been asked and are thinking seriously about it.
3. Never refuse to answer a question or fall back on that last resort of the stone-waller – 'No comment'. Both silence and a refusal to respond make it sound as if you have something to hide. If you lack the knowledge to reply, then say so, explain why and offer to come back with an answer in a short time. If you make that promise then be sure to keep it.
4. Never repeat a negative, it will only make it more memorable. As I have already suggested, use neutral terms such as points, issues, matter and so on.
5. If you don't know then say so. Never try and bluff your way, as chances are you'll be caught out and your whole credibility blown. Just say 'I don't know' and move on or, as above, tell the questioner you will find out.
6. Never agree with or start a debate with an aggressive questioner, since all you'll do is offer them a platform to

air their views. Simply note that people hold different opinions on that particular point and move the discussion along.

Persistence Often Pays

Even if the worst happens and you fail to win the business immediately, never assume that all is lost. Persistence is one of the essential skills of selling and the presentation is never over until a contract has been signed.

Says Paul Cowen of advertising agency CKT:

'What you never do is accept you've lost it. A good example of this was when my agency was pitching for Air UK. In the first presentation we pitched press and poster ideas, and the client actually wanted TV. We felt it was the right strategy for that client. It was very strong work but they wanted television and so they told us they were about to appoint another agency. I said to the marketing director, before you do this you should see the work for TV that we've done.

'We got him to hold over his decision to appoint the other agency and we pitched our TV work. Unfortunately he didn't like it, rang us the next day and said he still wasn't happy but he liked us. So we told him we'd got some other thoughts and would like to meet him again as it was a terribly important appointment for his company.

'He was flying abroad the next morning so we agreed to meet at Heathrow. We prepared another campaign overnight, went to the airport and presented our work to him. He still didn't feel comfortable with it.'

Even then CKT didn't give up. They talked Air UK's marketing director into letting them research the most appropriate form of advertising with potential consumers.

'The principle of the story is, never give up,' says Paul Cowan. 'That guy gave us many, many opportunities and any one of them could have come off.'

ACTION PLAN 16

As an exercise consider a client you know well and rate him or her for status and self-esteem.

The next time you are visiting a new client keep your eyes, and ears, out for the points listed below. Use this insight to determine the best way of managing the impression you make on that individual.

RATING BUYER'S STATUS

Rate these six status indicators on a scale of 1 to 5, where 1 = 'little or none' and 5 = 'as much as possible'.

1. How much privacy does he or she enjoy at work?
Partitioned areas in a general office, usually, indicate lower status than private rooms, while desk space in an open plan office normally shows the least status.

2. Where is their office located?
Penthouse suites or spacious rooms occupying a high, corner location in a tall building, enjoy the highest rating. An office next to the chief executive, managing director or chairman suggests status only slightly short of overall control.

3. How long can he or she keep subordinates waiting?
An unwritten but widely observed rule suggests that fifteen minutes is the longest anyone of equivalent or greater status will wait, unless there is a good reason for the delay.

4. How many personal possessions are there in the office?
The more you see displayed, the greater control that person has over their office space and the higher their status.

Personal items such as family photographs, hanging on the wall, rate as more significant than similar items on the desk.

5. How luxurious is the decor?
The greater an employee's status the more money a company is prepared to spend keeping them happy. Observe the size and style of desk, any antique or expensive modern furnishing, thickness of the carpet, type of wall covering and so on. The larger and more numerous the windows, and the more attractive the view, the higher their status.

6. Which way does the person face when behind their desk?
A chair positioned so the person looks out of a window demonstrates higher status than an office in which the individual faces the door. In commercial organisations only those with high status are sufficiently self-assured not to want to construct a barrier between themselves and their visitors.

Rating status
Total the score on as many of these status indicators as possible and refer to the table below. There is a maximum of thirty points if you managed to rate all the indicators above.

In many circumstances, you will only be able to obtain information about some of the factors. If so, calculate their percentage score against the possible maximum.

If, for instance, you were able to make only 3

observations (possible maximum rating 15) and this gave a rating of 9 points, then the percentage would be $9/30 \times 100 = 30\%$.

Percentage of Maximum Possible Score	*Status*
90–100	Very high
70–89	High
50–69	Moderate
30–49	Low
Less than 30	Very low

While these rules will prove mostly accurate in large, commercial organisations, they are less valid in government offices where such things as decor and furnishings are laid down by bureaucratic rules.

Here it is necessary to seek out more subtle signs of status. Is the floor carpeted? If so, does the carpet extend to the skirting boards or stop short?

Even a few inches less floor covering between two managers may betray a significant difference in their status.

Since many smaller companies are unable to afford the status symbols senior management in larger organisations come to expect as their right, you must be on the look-out for relative degrees of privileges.

These might include a desk larger than anyone else's or coffee served in china cups when others make do with plastic.

DETERMINING SELF-ESTEEM

Observe how often the person:

1. makes self-deprecating jokes;
2. boasts;

3. claims credit for something which, it seems clear, was largely the responsibility of others;
4. shifts the blame when something goes wrong, even though personally at fault;
5. goes mad over a trivial blunder by a subordinate;
6. behaves in a petty or vindictive manner;
7. insists they are right despite clear evidence to the contrary;
8. is rude or aggressive to a subordinate;
9. makes a spiteful remark about a colleague or competitor;
10. demonstrates a lack of concern for those working with him or her.

Each of these actions represents a negative point, suggesting a lack of self-esteem. Although trivial in themselves, when present in significant numbers, they are reliable signs of low self-esteem.

KEY POINTS

- You seldom get a second chance to make a first impression. The first four minutes of an initial meeting can be critical to your chances of success.
- Manage the impression you make by identifying and matching the customer's status and self-esteem.
- Dress to conform to the expectations of your customers. Be seen as a team player.
- Catch and hold your audience's attention right from the start. But avoid risky gimmicks which may backfire.
- Communicate energy and enthusiasm.

- Deal with objections in a positive and confident manner. They often provide sales openings.
- Avoid mistakes through careful planning. Never take anything for granted.
- By reading the buy signs you will have a better idea when to close.
- Do not treat questions and answers as a formality. They are a final chance to impress your customer.

STAGE FIVE

Creating Lifetime Customer Loyalty

'CUSTOMER CARE has much in common with sex.

Everyone is for it – Under certain conditions of course. Everyone feels they understand it – Even though they wouldn't want to have to explain it.

Everyone thinks its execution is only a matter of following one's natural inclinations – After all we do all get along somehow.

And, of course, everyone feels that all the problems in these areas are caused by other people – If only they would take the time to do things right.'

Philip Crosby, Quality Is Free

'CLEARLY DEFINE the long-range goals you aspire to, and all the obstacles in your way will become hills instead of mountains.'

O.A. Battista

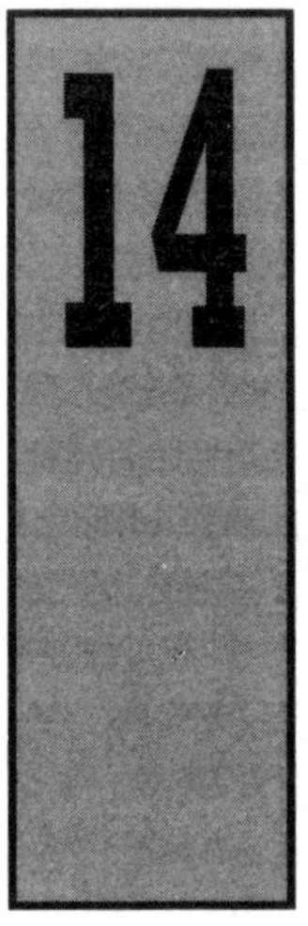

14 WINNING NEW BUSINESS FOR LIFE

'A SAILOR was leaning over the deck rail when an officer rushed up: 'Quick,' he cried, 'the ship is sinking!'

'So what?' the sailor shrugged. 'It's not my ship!'

WHILE ON a lecture tour I arrived at my hotel later than expected and asked the manager if it was possible to have dinner. 'No you bloody can't,' was his curt reply. 'All my staff are away on customer care courses!'

Customer care, like Total Quality Management, has become one of the business buzz terms of the last few years. Unfortunately, despite the millions of words written and spoken about caring for customers, it still appears to be far more talked about than practised.

While a survey – 'Your Company and Customer Care'

by Smith, Bundy and Partners, 1993 – among the marketing directors from over 3,000 top UK companies found that the vast majority saw customer care as essential for winning and retaining customers, many paid only lip-service to the concept.

Their ideas of what such a programme entailed was limited and naïve, with less than a quarter even bothering to measure customer satisfaction.

More than half cited product quality and competitive pricing as their chief priorities. By contrast, telephone response, delivery, dealing with complaints and training front-line staff were seen as far less significant.

Relationship marketing, designed to target specific products and services to individual customers, was consistently rated as an 'insignificant' aspect of customer care programmes.

Yet research shows neither quality nor pricing are the chief reasons why customers take their business elsewhere. Only 14 per cent change suppliers because of dissatisfaction with quality and a further 9 per cent are tempted away by lower prices. More than two-thirds, however, remove their custom as a result of 'an attitude of indifference' on the part of their suppliers.

While both quality and price are extremely important, what keeps customers loyal is being treated as individuals.

The simple secret of customer retention is customer satisfaction.

What Your Customers Really Want

Recent studies (such as Parasuraman, A. Berry, L. L. Zeithaml, 'Understanding Customer Expectations of Service', *Sloan Management Review* Vol. 32, No. 3, Spring 1991, pp. 39–48) have shown that customers will accept two levels of service – desired and adequate.

The desired level is the service customers hope to find. It is a blend of what they believe *can* and *should* be provided.

The adequate level is that which customers will accept without complaint.

Between these is a zone of tolerance. This varies from customer to customer and, potentially, from one purchasing situation to another for the same customer.

SERVICE LEVEL EXPECTATIONS

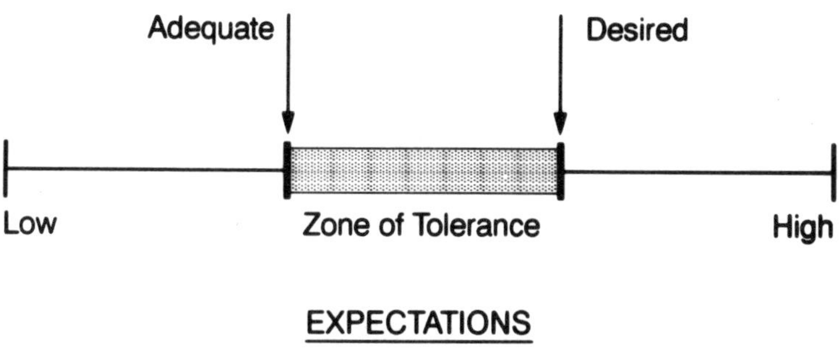

Among the factors influencing the extent of the tolerance zone are as follows.

- **Customer sophistication.** The more a consumer knows what can and ought to be achieved the greater their expectations. A guest who rarely stays at a hotel, for example, may have a lower level of expectation than an experienced business traveller. One consumer told researchers: 'As I've grown and learned more, I now have more to compare with.'
- **Availability.** At times of scarcity people have much lower expectations and a wider zone of tolerance than during periods of plenty. 'When your options are limited you take the best you can get,' one consumer told the

researchers. 'My expectations are not necessarily lower but my tolerance level is higher.'

- **The urgency of the situation.** In an emergency we expect and demand the best. If you are taken ill for example, second-rate medical treatment is entirely unacceptable.
- **Price.** The more we pay the greater our expectations for the service provided and the narrower our zone of tolerance. When flying first class across the Atlantic you expect to be treated better than those travelling economy.

Outcome and Process Dimensions

There are two aspects to delivering any type of product or service.

The first, called the outcome dimension, deals with the suitability and reliability of what is sold.

A customer, not unreasonably, expects a purchase to perform dependably and in accordance with its specifications.

If you buy the services of a travel agency, you expect them to book the tickets asked for on the correct flights and within your budget.

Suppliers receive no special appreciation for satisfying outcome dimensions, only criticisms if they fail to do so.

The second element is the process dimension. This is the *manner* in which a product or service is delivered and has four components.

1. **Tangibles.** Everything your customer sees, hears or touches, including the appearance of company offices or showrooms, retail premises, reception and bedrooms in hotels, plus sales and advertising literature.

   Ask yourself: 'Do customers feel comfortable when they call to see us?'; 'Are our premises attractive and welcoming?'; Does the atmosphere communicate a strong desire to do business, or is it unwelcoming and depressing?'

2. **Responsiveness.** The speed with which your customers' needs are met and the willingness of your staff to help. Do they go beyond what customers might reasonably expect by providing a superior service?

   Not long ago, while presenting a talk on customer care at the Registry Resort in Naples, Florida, I found I'd forgotten an adaptor to charge my electric shaver, in the bathroom socket. I called into the hotel shop to buy one. After apologising for not stocking the plug the assistant phoned around the hotel, located an adaptor and arranged for me to pick it up at the front desk.
3. **Assurance.** The knowledge and expertise possessed by your staff, their courtesy in addressing customer needs and the trust and confidence they convey to customers.
4. **Empathy.** The customers' beliefs that they are being listened to and understood by the supplier. That the attention they receive is genuinely caring and tailored to meet their specific needs.

How We Judge Outcome and Service Dimensions

Of necessity customers judge outcome dimensions only after the product or service has been *delivered*. After all, you can't know whether a product or service is reliable and suitable except by using it. There is no choice but to suck it and see.

Because customers are in a position to judge process dimensions (tangibles, responsiveness, assurance and empathy) *while* the service is being delivered, these are the most important factors in *meeting* and *exceeding* your customers' expectations.

Your Company Can Function at Three Service Levels

Firms can operate at a competitive disadvantage, a competitive advantage or a customer franchise level.

The Results of Customer Perceptions of Service Performance

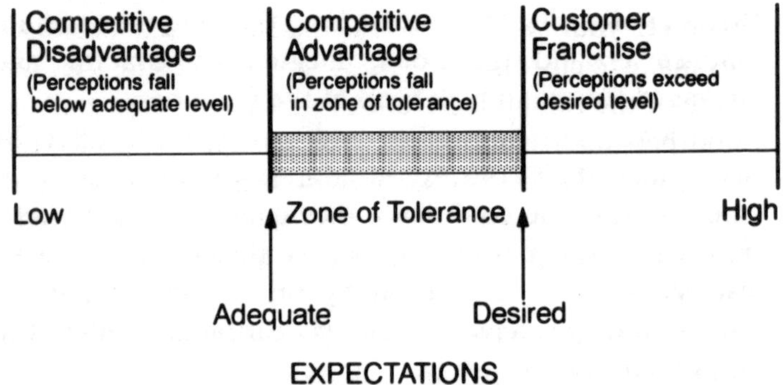

Customers of firms at a competitive disadvantage will be disloyal and eager to change suppliers whenever the opportunity arises.

Those operating at a competitive advantage enjoy a measure of loyalty, but their position is far from stable. Customers can still be lured away by competitors able to demonstrate that they offer a higher service.

The only way to win business for life is to franchise your customers by so consistently providing a superior service that they become virtually extensions of your own company, also giving you their unwavering loyalty by bringing in new business through recommendation.

Franchising your customers involves consistently performing at the desired level while seizing every opportunity to exceed that level.

Eight Ways to Franchise Your Customers

1. Be consistently reliable by nurturing a 'do it right first time' culture within your company.
2. Manage promises. Underpromising reduces your competitive advantage, while overpromising raises expectations beyond your ability to meet them.

   In the long term each is equally damaging to customer loyalty.
3. Empower your staff to follow through on any promises they make to customers. At the same time ensure they are aware of the full implications of what is being promised.
4. Build personal relationships with customers to increase their commitment. You could record a buyer's birthday and send them a card. This is far more memorable than the routine sending of company cards at Christmas or New Year.
5. Create open channels of communication so as to learn more about your customers and any problems they may have in relation to the service you provide.

   Scandinavian Airlines System, for example, put their marketing people behind ticket counters in order to meet passengers face-to-face.
6. Dealing with complaints promptly, courteously and empathically is crucial for ensuring customer loyalty.

   A study by Avis has shown that of the customers who experienced no problems with their service, 92 per cent use them again. Among those who have a problem this proportion falls to 78 per cent. Of those customers who made a complaint and felt satisfied by the way it was handled 91 per cent said they would use them again. But among those who complained and remained dissatisfied less than half said they would do so.

   Research among eleven European companies has shown that around 3 per cent of transactions lead to complaints. However, it also found that 45 per cent of transactions which were causing problems never led to any complaint. Instead the dissatisfied customers simply changed suppliers without ever explaining why. But the fact that they did not voice their complaint directly to the company did not mean they kept quiet about it. Disgruntled customers grumbled to twice as many people as satisfied customers spoke to about good service they received. And at least one customer was lost for every fifty hearing negative word-of-mouth advertising.

How to handle complaints

Never take complaints about your company personally. No matter how angry or aggressive the customer, try to stay calm.

Attempting to reason with an angry caller – or stop them in mid-flow – is useless, even when they've got their facts wrong. Much of their irritation will be defused if you listen sympathetically. Being a good listener turns you into a good friend.

As I suggested in the last chapter, when discussing how to deal with any objections at the end of your sales presentation, encourage the customer to voice *all* their complaints before you try and deal with any of them. This prevents them finding something fresh to complain about just when you felt the problem was resolved.

Restate their complaint in your own words in order to clarify the problem while reducing the customer's emotional attachment to it.

Take whatever action is appropriate. If you cannot find the answer straight away and promise to call back, make sure you do. If you promise prompt redress, be certain that such action is taken.

Complaints dealt with promptly and efficiently can *enhance* customer loyalty. They provide an opportunity for demonstrating your company's ability to deliver a superior service on process dimensions.

But a mishandled complaint is very likely to transform a previously loyal customer into a saboteur of your company's reputation.

7. Involve your whole staff in delivering superior process service. This can only be achieved by making them feel a sense of personal responsibility for your company's success. Unlike the sailor in the story which started this chapter, they must be made to feel it is 'their' ship.

8. Remember you do not have to win big to win everything. When Jan Carlzon took over the debt-ridden Scandinavian Airline Systems he realised there was nothing the company could do 1,000 per cent better. 'So,' he says, 'we decided to find a thousand things we could do 1 per cent better.'

   Be constantly on the look out for small things you can do just that little bit better.

   Winning the business for life does not involve being 1,000 per cent or even 100 per cent better than your competitors.

   Even a few points' difference in your ability to exceed customer expectations will be sufficient to secure their loyalty for life.

Putting this Plan into Practice

This book is based on more than twenty years' practical experience in sales psychology and management consultancy.

The procedures described have been tried and tested by some of the world's most successful companies operating in some of the world's most competitive markets.

They can and will work for your business equally well, but only if you have the enthusiasm, determination and persistence to put them into practice.

My hobby is sky-diving and when leaping from an aircraft many thousands of feet above the earth one thought is usually uppermost in my mind: ‘It won’t mean a thing if I don’t pull the string!’

When it comes to winning new business the same holds just as true.

BIBLIOGRAPHY

Ailes, R., *You are the Message*, Illinois: Dow Jones-Irwin, 1988.

Alexander, R., *Power Speech*, New York: American Management Association, 1986.

Aronson, S., *Everyone's Guide to: Opening Doors by Telephone*, Laguna Hills: Talmud Press, 1981.

Arredondo, L., *How to Present Like a Pro: Getting People to See Things Your Way*, New York: McGraw-Hill Inc., 1991.

Atkinson, P.E., *Creating Culture Change: The Key to Successful Total Quality Management*, Kempston: IFS Ltd, 1990.

Beer, M., *Break the Rules in Selling*, London: Mercury Books, 1991.

Bender, P.U., *Secrets of Power Presentations*, Toronto: The Achievement Group, 1991.

Bernstein, D., *Put It Together, Put It Across*, London: Cassell Publishers Ltd, 1988.

Bowman, L., *High Impact Business Presentations*, London: Business Books Ltd., 1991.

Brown, A., *Customer Care Management*, London: Heinemann Ltd, 1989.

Bullmore, J., *Behind the Scenes in Advertising*, Henley-on-Thames: NTC Publications Ltd, 1991.

Burley-Allen, M., *Listening: The Forgotten Skill*, New York: John Wiley and Sons Inc., 1982.

Chaudhry-Lawton, R. and Lawton, R., *Ignition: Sparking Organizational Change*, London: BCA, 1992.

Chisnall, P.M., *Marketing: A Behavioural Analysis*, London: McGraw-Hill Book Company, 1985.

Chisnall, P.M., *The Essence of Marketing Research*, London: Prentice Hall International Ltd, 1991.

Chisnall P.M., *Marketing Research*, London: McGraw Hill Book Company, 1992.

Curry, J., *Know Your Customers*, London: Kogan Page Ltd, 1992.

Denny, R., *Selling to Win*, London: Kogan Page Ltd, 1988.

Di Salvo, V., *Business and Professional Communication*, Ohio: Charles E. Merrill Publishing Company, 1977.

Fisher, R. and Ury, W., *Getting to Yes*, London: Hutchinson Business, 1986.

Fishman, D.B. and Cherniss, C., *The Human Side of Corporate Competitiveness*, London: Sage Publications Ltd, 1990.

Fletcher, W., *A Glittering Haze*, Henley-on-Thames: NTC Publications Ltd, 1992.

Forbes Ley, D., *The Best Seller*, London: Kogan Page Ltd, 1989.

Goldzimer, L.S., *Customer Driven*, London: Hutchinson Business Books Ltd, 1989.

Golis, C.C., *Empathy Selling*, London: Kogan Page Ltd, 1991.

Good, B., *Telephone Selling Techniques that Really Work*, London: Piatkus Books, 1986.

Hamlin, S., *How to Talk so People Listen*, Wellingborough: Thorsons Publishers Ltd, 1989.

Harvey, C., *Secrets of the World's Top Sales*, London: Business Books Ltd, 1989.

Heller, R., *The Business of Winning*, London: Sidgwick and Jackson, 1980.

Heller, R., *The New Naked Manager*, London: Hodder and Stoughton, 1985.

Henzell-Thomas, N. and Peoples, D.A., *Super-Charge Your Selling*, London: Hutchinson Business Books Ltd, 1989.

Henzell-Thomas, N., *Sales Master Class*, London: Hutchinson Business Books Ltd, 1990.

Hirokawa, R.Y., and Poole, M.S., *Communication and Group Decision Making*, London: Sage Publications Ltd, 1986.

Hughes, S., *Professional Presentations*, Sydney: McGraw-Hill Book Company, 1990.

Kennedy, G., *Everything is Negotiable*, London: Business Books Ltd, 1982.

King, N., *The Last Five Minutes*, New York: Prentice Hall Press, 1990.

Kushel, G., *The 4%*, London: Sidgwick and Jackson, 1985.

Lancaster, G., *The 20% Factor*, Vermont: David and Charles Publishers, 1987.

Lane, R.E., *The Market Experience*, Cambridge: Cambridge University Press, 1991.

LeBoeuf, M., *How to Motivate People*, London: Sidgwick and Jackson, 1986.

Leeds, D., *Powerspeak*, London: Piatkus Books, 1988.

Le Poole, S., *Never Take No for an Answer*, London: Kogan Page Ltd, 1987.

Lewis, D., *The Secret Language of Success*, London: Bantam Books, 1989

Lewis, D., *One Minute Stress Management*, London: Heinemann Ltd, 1993.

McDonald, C., *How Advertising Works*, Henley-on-Thames: NTC Publications Ltd, 1992.

McDonald, M. and Leppard J.W., *Marketing by Matrix*, London: Butterworth-Heinemann Ltd, 1992.

McDonald, M. and Leppard J.W., *How to Sell a Service*, London: Heinemann Ltd, 1986.

Meyer, M.W. and Zucker, L.G., *Permanently Failing Organizations*, London: Sage Publications Ltd, 1989.

Mills, H.A., Negotiate: *The Art of Winning*, London: BCA, 1991.

Pickens, J.W., *The Art of Closing a Deal*, London: Prion, 1989.

Rickards, T., *Stimulating Innovation: A Systems Approach*, London: Frances Pinter Publishers Ltd, 1985.

Roman, K. and Maas, J., *How to Advertise: What Works, What Doesn't and Why*, London: Kogan Page Ltd, 1976.

Shook, R.L., The Art of the Hard Sell, London: Piatkus Books, 1990.

Vroom, V.H. and Deci, E.L., *Management and Motivation*, London: Penguin Group, 1970.

Weymes, P., *How to Perfect Your Selling Skills*, London: Kogan Page Ltd, 1990.

Wille, E., *Quality: Achieving Excellence*, London: Century Business, 1992.

Williams, K.C., *Behavioural Aspects of Marketing*, Oxford: Heinemann Ltd, 1981.

INDEX